MARRIAGES
OF
ISLE OF WIGHT COUNTY, VIRGINIA,
1628-1800

D1617263

By

BLANCHE ADAMS CHAPMAN

Reprinted in an Improved Format

With a New Index

By

ANITA COMTOIS

CLEARFIELD

Originally published
Smithfield, Virginia, 1933

Reprinted in an Improved Format
with a New Index
Genealogical Publishing Co., Inc.
Baltimore, Maryland, 1976, 1982

Reprinted for
Clearfield Company, Inc. by
Genealogical Publishing Co., Inc.
Baltimore, Maryland
1995, 1997, 1999, 2002

Library of Congress Cataloging in Publication Data
Chapman, Blanche Adams, 1895-
    Marriages of Isle of Wight County, Virginia, 1628-1800.
    Reprint of the 1933 ed. published in Smithfield, Va. under title: Isle
Wight County marriages, 1628-1800.
    Includes index.
    1. Isle of Wight Co., Va.—Genealogy. 2. Registers of births, etc.—
Isle of Wight Co., Va. I. Title.
F232.18C5   1976   929'.3755'54   75-29198
ISBN 0-8063-0710-2

The publisher gratefully acknowledges
the loan of the original volume from the
North Carolina State Library
Raleigh, North Carolina

Made in the United States of America

PREFACE

For several years I have been compiling a list of marriages of Isle of Wight County, Virginia. Because so few marriage bonds prior to the year 1800 survive, I feel that my list should be made available to the many researchers interested in this early county. The majority of these marriages can be verified from the references given; those which cannot may be assumed to derive from inference and deduction.

Few Isle of Wight families can be traced without regard to the records of Southampton County (Nottoway Parish), which was erected from Isle of Wight in 1749. The bonds in this county, for example, antedate the earliest Isle of Wight bond by twenty years, and a large number have better withstood the ravages of time. The references to marriages in Southampton County are not to bonds, however, but to other sources, for I feel that inferential marriage records founded upon will books and deed books are of greater value.

The dates given in the list are the dates of the papers in which proof of marriage is found. Where the evidence is not actually strong enough to prove a marriage, although I believe it to be sufficient, I have indicated as much by the symbol #. The book in the Isle of Wight archives known as the "Great Book" is composed of both deeds and wills. If the proof of marriage is found in the deeds, the reference if given as G. B.; if it is found in the wills, the reference is G. B. 2. The following abbreviations are uniform throughout: W. B. signifies Will Book, D. B., Deed Book, and O. B., Order Book.

Blanche Adams Chapman, Genealogist

CONTENTS

MARRIAGES

1628-1800

ABRAHAM, JOHN and ELIZABETH WASHINGTON, daughter of Arthur
Washington. 1758. Southampton County W. B. I,
p. 408.

ADAMS, JOHN and MARY WASHINGTON, daughter of Arthur Washington.
1769. Southampton County D. B. 4, p. 138.

ADAMS, THOMAS and MARY RAWLINGS, daughter of John Rawlings.
1778. Southampton County W. B. 3, p. 233.

#ALLEN, HENRY and MARY BOAZMAN, daughter of Ralph Boazman.
1693. G. B. p. 560. D. B. I, p. 66.

ALLEN, JOHN and ELIZABETH SELLOWAY, daughter of John Selloway.
1712. G. B. 2, p. 158.

ALLEN, THOMAS and MRS. MARTHA RUTTER, relict of Walter Rutter.
1704. W. & D. B. 2, p. 451, 522, 656.

#ALLEN, THOMAS and HONOUR FULLER, daughter of Ezekial Fuller.
1722. G. B. 2, p. 133. W. B. 4, p. 333.

ALLEY, THOMAS and MRS. MARY JENNINGS, relict of John Jennings.
1678. W. & D. B. 2, (Rev.), p. 45.

ALLMAND, AARON and ANN HARRISON, daughter of William Harrison.
1762. W. B. 7, p. 200. O. B. 1759-63, p. 393.

ALLMAND, ISAAC and MRS. MARY WIGGS, relict of George Wiggs.
1778. D. B. 13, p. 505.

APPLEWHAITE, ARTHUR and JANE MOSCROP, daughter of Thomas Moscrop.
1745. W. B. 5, p. 14. O. B. 1746-52, p. 310.

APPLEWHAITE, ARTHUR and RIDLEY WILSON, daughter of George Wilson.
1792. W. B. 6, p. 379. W. B. 10, p. 226. W. B. 11,
p. 21.

APPLEWHAITE, HENRY and ANN MARSHALL, daughter of Humphry Marshall.
1711. W. & D. B. 2, p. 533.

APPLEWHAITE, HENRY and SARAH MILLER, daughter of Nicholas Miller.
1779. W. B. 7, p. 133. O. B. 1772-80, p. 497.

APPLEWHAITE, MILLS and MARGARET HARRISON. 1786. Isle of Wight
Land Tax Books.

APPLEWHAITE, THOMAS and MARY ARCHER, daughter of Edward Archer of
Norfolk. 1764. D. B. 11, p. 214.

APPLEYARD, WILLIAM and MARGARET DODMAN, daughter of John Dodman of Mulberry Island. 1679. W. & D. B. I, p. 429.

ARRINGTON, WILLIAM and ELIZABETH PEDIN, daughter of James Pedin. 1703. D. B. I, p. 392.

ASKEW, JOHN and KATHERINE OGLETHORPE, daughter of Thomas Oglethorpe. 1694. D. B. I. (Rev.) p. 48. W. & D. B. 2, p. 292.

ASKEW, NICHOLAS and SARAH OGLETHROPE, daughter of Thomas Oglethrope. 1694. D. B. I. (Rev.) p. 48. W. & D. B. 2, p. 292.

ATKINS, CHRISTOPHER and ELIZABETH RODWELL, sister of John Rodwell. 1719. G. B. 2, p. 28.

ATKINS, DAVID and SUSANNAH EXUM, daughter of Robert Exum. 1751. D. B. 8, p. 422.

#ATKINSON, JAMES and MARY HOLLIMAN, daughter of Christopher Holliman. 1691. W. & D. B. 2, p. 309. G. B. 2, p. 146.

ATKINSON, JAMES JR. and MRS. MARTHA PRICE, relict of Joseph Price. 1739. D. B. 5, p. 360. W. B. 3, p. 133.

ATKINSON, JAMES and MARY ONEY, daughter of Leonard Oney. 1772. Southampton County W. B. 3, p. 251.

ATKINSON, JESSE and MARY WILSON, daughter of George Wilson. 1772. D. B. 12, p. 462. O. B. 1759-63, p. 151.

ATKINSON, JOHN and ANN HOLLIMAN, daughter of Christopher Holliman. 1691. W. & D. B. 2, p. 309. G. B. 2, p. 144.

ATKINSON, JOHN and ELIZABETH ONEY, daughter of Leonard Oney. 1772. Southampton County W. B. 3, p. 251.

ATKINSON, SIOMON and CELIA WOMBWELL, daughter of Thomas Wombwell. 1784. W. B. 9, p. 294.

AYRES, FRANCIS and MRS. JANE CLARK, relict of Humphry Clark. 1656. Bk. A. P. 61 & 70. W. & D. B. 2, p. 139.

BACON, NATHANIEL SR. and MRS. ANN SMITH. 1654. Bk. A., p.93.

BAGNALL, JAMES and ANN BRASWELL, daughter of Robert Braswell. 1667. W. & D. B. 2, p. 52. W. & D. B. I, p. 311.

BAGNALL, JAMES and REBECCA IZARD, daughter of Richard Izard. 1675. W. & D. B. 2, p. 135.

BAGNALL, NATHAN and ANN WILKINSON, daughter of Richard Wilkinson. 1741. W. B. 4, p. 418.

BAILEY, BARNEBY and MARY WOOD, daughter of George Wood. 1770. Southampton County W. B. 2, p. 342.

BAILEY, BENJAMIN and ELIZABETH SCOTT, daughter of William Scott. 1763. W. B. 7, p. 404.

BAILEY, JOHN and MARY CALTHORPE, daughter of Charles Calthorpe.

2

1756. Southampton County W. B. 2, p. 30.

BALDWIN, WILLIAM and MRS. ELIZABETH BARLOW, relict of Thomas
Barlow. 1679. W. & D. B. 2, p. 200. W. & D. B. I,
p. 405.

BAKER, BLAKE and CATHERINE BRIDGER, daughter of Joseph Bridger.
1786. Isle of Wight Land Tax Book 1786-87.

BAKER, CHARLES and ------- WILLIAMS, daughter of Rowland Williams.
1688. W. & D. B. 2, p. 71.

BAKER, RICHARD and JUDITH BRIDGER, daughter of Joseph Bridger.
1784. D. B. 15, p. 273.

BALLARD, ELISHA and ANN LAWRENCE, daughter of John Lawrence.
1757. W. B. 6, p. 313.

BARCROFT, JOSIAH and MARY WILSON, daughter of Sampson Wilson.
1804. W. B. 12, p. 21.

BARHAM, THOMAS and SARAH NEWSUM, daughter of Thomas Newsum.
1745. W. B. 5, p. 5.

BARLOW, GEORGE and SARAH CLAY, daughter of William Clay. 1694.
D. B. I. (Rev.) p. 68.

BARLOW, WILLIAM and LUCY LANCASTER, daughter of Henry Lancaster.
1784. W. B. 9, p. 276.

BARNES, JOHN and ANN JONES, daughter of John Jones. 1697.
W. & D. B. 2, p. 385.

BARRAUD,- PHILLIP of Williamsburg and ANN HANSFORD, daughter of
Lewis Hansford. 1786. W. B. 10, p. 44.

#BATT, WILLIAM and MRS. SARAH GEORGE, relict of William George.
1721. G. B. 2, p. 108.

BATTLE, JOHN and SARAH BROWNE, daughter of Dr. Samuel Browne.
1739. W. B. 4, p. 274.

BAYNTON, PETER and ELIZABETH BOUTCHER. 1669. D. B. I, p. 104.

#BEALE, BENJAMIN JR. and MARTHA NEVILLE, daughter of John Neville.
1689. D. B. I, p. 22.

BEALE, BENJAMIN and LYDIA RICKES, daughter of Abraham Rickes.
1748. D. B. 8, p. 124.

BEALE, JOHN and PATIENCE MAYO, daughter of William Mayo (May).
1745. D. B. 7, p. 154.

BECKETT, CHARLES and JANE JOHNSON, daughter of Thomas Johnson.
1671. W. & D. B. 2, p. 102.

BELL, BENJAMIN and MARY LANCASTER, daughter of Mrs. Sarah
Lancaster. 1722. G. B. 2, p. 125.

BELL, WILLIAM and ANN JONES, daughter of Richard Jones. 1721.
G. B. 2, p. 84.

BENN, JAMES and JANE SMITH, daughter of Arthur Smith. 1697.
W. & D. B. 2, p. 377 & 381.

3

BENN, JAMES and MARY APPLEWHAITE, daughter of Thomas Applewhaite.
1728. W. B. 3, p. 340 & 329. W. B. 4, p. 257.

BENNETT, AMBROSE and MARY IZARD, daughter of Richard Izard.
1675. W. & D. B. 2, p. 135.

BENNETT, MOSES and MRS. LUCY SIMMONS, relict of Stephen Simmons.
1769. Southampton County O. B. 5, p. 199.

BERRYMAN, ROBERT and MRS. MARY POWELL, relict of Nathan Powell.
1729. W. B. 3, p. 159 & 179.

BEST, HENRY and MRS. ELIZABETH GODWIN, relict of James Godwin.
1755. W. B. 5, p. 300. W. B. 6, p. 161.

BEST, JOHN and MARTHA HILL, daughter of Mrs. Silvestra Hill.
1693. D. B. I, p. 148.

BEVAN, HARDY and DORCAS DOYEL, daughter of Edward Doyel. 1762.
Southampton County W. B. I, p. 495.

#BEVAN, PETER and MARY GREEN, daughter of Mrs. Mary Green.
1734. W. B. 4, p. 108 & 197.

BEVAN, ROBERT and SARAH GROSS, daughter of Francis Gross. 1750.
W. B. 5, p. 365.

BIDGOOD, JOHN JR. and ANN LUPO, daughter of James Lupo. 1712.
W. & D. B. 2, p. 542. W. B. 3, p. 9.

BIDGOOD, WILLIAM SR. and HESTER WILLIAMSON, daughter of Geo.
Williamson. 1746. D. B. 7, p. 433. D. B. 9, p. 172.

BIDGOOD, WILLIAM and JANE INGRAM, daughter of Jennings Ingram.
1764. O. B. 1764-68, p. 1. W. B. 8, p. 308.

BLUNT, RICHARD and ------- CREWS, sister of John Crews. 1690.
D. B. I, p. 267.

BLUNT, RICHARD and MARY BROWNE, daughter of William Browne.
1709. W. & D. B. 2, p. 498.

BLUNT, WILLIAM and ELIZABETH BRESSIE, daughter of Hugh Bressie.
1749. W. B. 7, p. 126.

BOAZMAN, RALPH and MARY PRICE. 1723. G. B., p. 560

#BODDIE, WILLIAM and MRS. MARY GRIFFIN, relict of Owen Griffin.
1712. W. & D. B. 2, p. 633. W. B. 3, p. 299.

BOND, JOHN and ------- BELL, sister of John Bell. 1687.
W. & D. B. 2, p. 274.

BOWEN, JOHN and DORCAS RUNELS, daughter of Henry Runels (Reynolds). 1725. W. B. 3, p. 155.

BOYD, THOMAS and MRS. MARTHA NORSWORTHY, relict of Geo. Norsworthy. 1706. D. B. 2, p. 59.

BOYKIN, FRANCIS and ANN MARSHALL, daughter of John Marshall.
1783. W. B. 9, p. 232. D. B. 14, p. 193.

BOYKIN, WILLIAM and MARGARET VICKERS, daughter of Ralph Vickers.
1734. W. B. 4, p. 44. W. B. 5, p. 89.

4

BOULGER, THOMAS and SARAH SMITH, daughter of William Smith.
1704. W. & D. B. 2, p. 470 & 476.

BOURDEN, NICHOLAS and MRS. PRUDENCE WRENN, relict of John Wrenn.
1738. O. B. 1746-52, p. 229. W. B. 4, p. 250.

BRADDY, PATRICK and MARGARET WOOD, sister of Josias Wood.
1709. W. & D. B. 2, p. 497.

BRADLEY, DAVID and MRS. ELIZABETH HARRISON, relict of John
Harrison. 1790. W. B. 11, p. 199.

#BRADLEY, SAMUEL and MRS. MARY PITT, relict of John Pitt.
1759. O. B. 1759-63, p. 28. W. B. 7, p. 419.

BRADSHAW, WILLIAM and SELAH BOON, daughter of Ratcliff Boon.
1795. W. B. 11, p. 174 & 275.

BRAGG, JAMES and MARY EDWARDS, daughter of Robert Edwards.
1694. D. B. I, (Rev.) p. 57.

BRANCH, GEORGE of Surry County and ANNE ENGLAND, daughter of
Francis England. 1677. W. & D. B. 2, p. 144.

BRANTLEY, BENJAMIN and MARY LUPO, sister of Philip Lupo. 1772.
, W. B. 9, p. 30 & 127.

BRANTLEY, EDWARD and MARY DAVIS, sister of John Davis. 1750.
O. B. 1746-52, p. 229.

BRANTLEY, JOHN and ELIZABETH CLAY, daughter of William Clay.
1694. D. B. I, (Rev.) p. 68.

BRANTLEY, JOHN and MRS. ------ WILSON, relict of John Wilson.
1694. D. B. I, (Rev.) p. 81.

BRANTLEY, PHILIP and JOYCE LEWIS, sister of John Lewis. 1692.
W. & D. B. 2, p. 320.

BRANTLEY, PHILIP and MRS. MARY APPLEWHAITE, relict of Henry
Applewhaite, Jr. 1745. W. B. 4, p. 547.

BRANTLEY, WILLIS and MRS. MARY JENKINS, relict of Valentine
Jenkins. 1780. O. B. 1780-83, p. 115. W. B. 10, p. 189.

BRASSELL, JOHN and MRS. JANE LEWIS, relict of Zebulon Lewis.
1741. W. B. 4, p. 229 & 396.

BRESSIE, (BRASSIEUR, BRACEY) JOHN and MARY PITT, daughter of
Robt. Pitt. 1672. W. & D. B. 2, p. 128.

BRESSIE, JOHN of Nansemond County and MARTHA NORSWORTHY, daughter
of George Norsworthy. 1738. W. B. 4, p. 221 & 375.
D. B. 5, p. 48.

BRESSIE, SOLOMON and ------- HAILE, daughter of John Haile.
1792. W. B. 10, p. 297.

BREWER, JOHN and MRS. JOANNA CANNADAY, relict of Samuel Cannaday.
1711. W. & D. B. 2, p. 517 & 521.

BRICKELL, MATHAIS and RACHEL NOYALL. 1750. D. B. 8, p. 337.

BRIDGER, JOHN and MRS. ------- DICKENSON, relict of Christopher
Dickenson. 1739. W. B. 4, p. 71.

5

BRIDGER, JOHN and MARTHA MALLORY, daughter of John Mallory.
1788. W. B. 10, p. 128 & 129.

BRIDGER, JOSEPH and HESTER PITT, daughter of Robert Pitt.
1672. W. & D. B. 2, p. 128.

BRIDGER, JOSEPH and ELIZABETH NORSWORTHY, daughter of John
Norseworthy. 1691. W. & D. B. 2, p. 310 & 574.

BRIDGER, JOSEPH and ------- PITT, daughter of John Pitt. 1729.
W. B. 4, p. 43.

BRIDGER, JOSEPH and SARAH DAVIS, daughter of John Davis.
1754. D. B. 9, p. 272.

BRIDGER, LEAR and ------- GLOVER, daughter of William Glover.
W. B. 6, p. 525. W. B. 9, p, 272.

BRIDGER, SAMUEL and MRS. ELIZABETH WOORY, relict of Joseph
Woory. 1693. W. & D. B. 2, p. 336.

BRIDGER, WILLIAM and ELIZABETH ALLEN, sister of Joseph Allen.
1727. W. B. 3, p. 15 & 68.

BRIDGER, WILLIAM and MARTHA SMITH, daughter of Arthur Smith.
1732. W. B. 3, p. 309. W. B. 4, p. 424.

BRIGGS, CHARLES and ELIZABETH BLOW, daughter of Samuel Blow.
1766. Southampton County W. B. 2, p. 166.

BRIGGS, JAMES SR. and SARAH EDWARDS, daughter of Charles Edwards.
1713. W. & D. B. 2, p. 578.

BRIGGS, JAMES and MRS. MARY BELL. Marriage contract. 1723.
G. B., p. 569.

BRITT, EDWARD SR. and SARAH JOHNSON, daughter of Robert Johnson.
1757. W. B. 6, p. 304. Southampton County W. B. 4,
p. 372.

BRITT, JOHN and SUSANNAH BRESSIE, daughter of Hugh Bressie.
1699. D. B. I, p. 277. W. B. 3, p. 20.

BROCK, ROBERT and MRS. SUSSANNAH TOULE, relict of Hercules
Toule. 1685. W. & D. B. 2, p. 244.

BROCK, THOMAS and SUSANNAH HOUSE. 1756. D. B. 14, (Rev.)
p. 169.

BROMFIELD, JOHN and MRS. OLIVE DRIVER, relict of Giles Driver.
1679. W. & D. B. I, p. 431. W. & D. B. 2, p. 454.

BROWN, EDWARD and MRS. ------- CULLEY, relict of John Culley.
1690. W. & D. B. 2, (Rev.) p. 74.

BROWN, GEORGE and MARY HOLLIDAY, daughter of Samuel Holliday.
1762. O. B. 1759-63, p. 342.

BROWN, JAMES of London and HESTER NASH, daughter of Nicholas
Nash. 1730. D. B. 4, p. 182.

BROWN, DR. JESSE and ELIZABETH RIDLEY, daughter of Nathaniel
Ridley. 1750. W. B. 5, p. 322.

BROWN, JESSE and ESTHER STEPHENSON, daughter of Thomas

Stephenson. 1770. Southampton County W. B. 2, p. 314.

BROWN, JOHN and MARY BODDIE, daughter of William Boddie.
1682. W. & D. B. 2, p. 231.

#BROWN, JOHN and ------- WILLIAMS, daughter of John Williams Sr.
1692. W. & D. B. 2, p. 318. G. B. 2, p. 90.

BROWN, JOHN and MRS. HANNAH HOLLIDAY, relict of Samuel Holliday.
1762. O. B. 1759-63, p. 342.

BROWN, JOHN and ------- PITT, sister of Isham Pitt. 1794.
W. B. 10, p. 306.

BROWN, SAMUEL and ELIZABETH PITT, daughter of John Pitt. 1759.
O. B. 1759-63, p. 28. W. B. 7, p. 419.

BROWN, THOMAS and ANN WENTWORTH, daughter of Samuel Wentworth.
1767. D. B. 15, p. 140.

BROWN, WILLIAM and ------- WOOD, sister of Josias Wood. 1682.
W. & D. B. 2, p. 232.

BROWN, WILLIAM and SARAH EDWARDS, daughter of Benjamin Edwards.
1761. Southampton County D. B. 3, p. 80.

BROWN, WILLIAM and ANN TAYLOR, daughter of Mrs. Lucy Taylor.
1776. Southampton County W. B. 3, p. 151.

BRUCE, JAMES and MARGARET THROPE, daughter of Timothy Thrope.
1750. Southampton County W. B. I, p. 37.

BRUIN, THOMAS and ------- MADISON, daughter of Mrs. Ann Madison.
1670. W. & D. B. 2, p. 109.

BRYANT, CHARLES and LYDIA MONRO, daughter of John Monro.
1760. W. B. 7, p. 22. O. B. 1760-68, p. 244.

BRYANT, EDWARD and CHRISTIAN COUNCIL, daughter of Hodges Council.
1699. D. B. 4, p. 104. W. & D. B. 2, p. 419.

BRYANT, GEORGE and MRS. SARAH WILLS, relict of John Wills.
1764. O. B. 1764-68, p. 11. W. B. 7, p. 335.

BRYANT, JOHN and ELIZABETH JOYNER, daughter of Bridgman Joyner.
1716. G. B. 39.

BRYANT, JOHN and MARY MONRO, daughter of John Monro. 1760.
W. B. 7, p. 22.

BULGER, THOMAS and MRS. ELIZABETH WRIGHT, relict of Thomas
Wright. 1680. W. & D. B. 2, p. 208.

BULGER, THOMAS and SARAH SMITH, daughter of William Smith.
1704. W. & D. B. 2, p. 470.

BULLOCK, JOHN and SALLY BRIDGER, daughter of Samuel Bridger.
1797. O. B. 8, p. 25.

BULLOCK, JOSEPH and PENELOPE DIXON, daughter of Thomas Dixon.
1746. W. B. 5, p. 141.

BULLOCK, JOSEPH and PENELOPE GARNER, daughter of John Garner.
1761. W. B. 7, p. 184 & 194.

7

BULLOCK, THOMAS and MRS. MARY ALLEN, relict of Henry Allen.
1695. D. B. I, p. 166.

BULLOCK, WILLIAM and RACHELL NEVELLE, daughter of Roger Nevelle.
1775. D. B. 13, p. 325.

BULLOCK, WILLIS and MARY NEWMAN, daughter of John Newman.
1782. W. B. 9, p. 172 & 273.

BUNKLEY, JACOB and MARY HOLLIDAY, daughter of Mrs. Ann Holliday.
1760. O. B. 1759-63, p. 144.

BUNKLEY, JOSHUA and SALLY KING, daughter of Mrs. Martha King.
1783. W. B. 10, p. 202.

BURK, THOMAS and SALLY HARRISON, sister of William Harrison.
1769. W. B. 8, p. 22.

BURNETT, ROBERT and MRS. JEAN WILLIAMSON, relict of Dr. Robert
Williamson. 1672. W. & D. B. 2, p. 85 & 116.

BUTLER, JOHN and SARAH WRIGHT, sister of John Wright. 1753.
W. B. 6, p. 297 & 400.

BUTLER, JOHN and MRS. MARY HARRIS, relict of Mathew Harris.
1801. W. B. 11, p. 441.

BUTLER, STEPHEN and SALLY MARSHALL, daughter of Dempsey Marshall.
1805. O. B. 1803-1806, p. 371.

CALCOTE, ------- and ANN BROMFIELD, daughter of John Bromfield.
1734. D. B. 4, p. 397.

CALCOTE (CALCLOUGH), JAMES and MARY GOODRICH, daughter of George
Goodrich. 1750. D. B. 8, p. 349.

CARR, NATHAN and ANN ENGLISH, daughter of Mrs. Mary English.
1763. D. B. 11, p. 186.

CARR, ROBERT and ------- LAWRENCE, daughter of John Lawrence.
1738. W. B. 4, p. 226.

CARR, ROBERT and ELIZABETH VASSER, daughter of Nathan Vasser.
1770. Southampton County W. B. 2, p. 320.

CARRELL, GRAY and ------- JONES, daughter of David Jones.
W. B. 10, p. 313. W. B. 11, p. 41.

#CARRELL, JOHN and ELIZABETH VASSER, daughter of Peter Vasser.
1708. W. & D. B. 2, p. 297 & 585.

CARRELL, JOHN and MARY WHEADON, daughter of James Wheadon.
1760. O. B. 1759-60, p. 195.

CARRELL, THOMAS and MRS. JANE VICARS, relict of John Vicars.
1680. W. & D. B. 2, p. 208.

CARRELL, THOMAS and MARY HOUSE, daughter of Robert House. 1704.
D. B. I, p. 419.

CARSTAPHEN, PERKINS and BETTY SAUNDERS, daughter of Robert
Saunders. 1792. W. B. 10, p. 270.

CARTER, THOMAS and MAGDALEN MOORE, daughter of George Moore.
1673. D. B. I, p. 324.

CARTER, WILLIAM of Dinwiddie County and MARY LANE, daughter of
Richard Lane. 1760. Southampton County D. B. 3, p. 6.

CARTER, WILLIAM and MRS. MARY SMITH, relict of Joseph Smith.
1779. W. B. 10, p. 103. W. B. 11, p. 116.

CARVER, WILLIAM and JANE MOORE, daughter of John Moore. 1692.
D. B. I, p. 46.

CASEY, NICHOLAS and CONSTANT HARRISON, daughter of John Harrison.
1732. W. B. 3, p. 318.

CASEY, RICHARD and JANE REYNOLDS, daughter of Richard Reynolds.
1706. D. B. 2, p. 46.

CASEY, THOMAS and MRS. HANNAH PARR, relict of Anthony Parr.
1779. O. B. 1772-80, p. 490.

CHAMPION, JOHN and MRS. DIAN BARNES, relict of Thomas Barnes.
1683. W. & D. B. 2, p. 235.

CHANNELL, ARTHUR and PEGGY BOWDEN, daughter of Lemuel Bowden.
1804. O. B. 1803-1806, p. 118.

CHANNELL, RALPH and MRS. GRACE PERRY, relict of Phillip Perry.
1669. W. & D. B. 2, (Rev.) p. 22.

CHANNELL, THOMAS and ELIZABETH MONTGOMERY. 1763. O. B.
1759-63, p. 431.

#CHAPMAN, CHARLES and ANN DAY, sister of James Day. 1700.
W. & D. B. 2, p. 428 & 475.

CHAPMAN, CHARLES and ANN PARKER, daughter of Thomas Parker.
1741. W. B. 4, p. 422. W. B. 5, p. 235.

CHAPMAN, JOHN and FRANCES WARD, daughter of Thomas Ward.
1702. D. B. 2, p. 15. W. & D. B. 2, p. 333.

CHAPMAN, JOHN and JORDAN HARRISON, daughter of William Harrison.
1751. D. B. 8, p. 401.

CHAPMAN, JOHN and SARAH WIGGS, daughter of George Wiggs. 1778.
D. B. 13, p. 505.

CHAPMAN, RICHARD and MRS. ESTHER WOODWARD, relict of John G.
Woodward. 1802. O. B. 1801-3, p. 360.

CHAPMAN, WILLIAM and MARY CROCKER, daughter of William Crocker.
1778. O. B. 1772-80, p. 425.

CHILDS, THOMAS and ------- JACKSON, daughter of John Jackson.
1762. W. B. 7, p. 121.

CLARK, JAMES and JUDITH HUNTT, daughter of William Huntt.
1669. W. & D. B. 2, p. 78 & 110.

CLARK, HENRY and MRS. JANE AYRES, relict of Francis Ayres.
1679. W. & D. B. 2, p. 191.

CLARK, JOHN and MARY FLAKE, daughter of Robert Flake. 1670.
W. & D. B. 2, p. 89.

9

CLARK, JOHN and REBECCA RICHARDSON, daughter of William Richardson. 1764. O. B. 1764-68, p. 281 & 394.

CLARK, JOHN and SARAH BEMBRIDGE GODWIN, daughter of Mrs. Sarah Godwin. 1767. D. B. 12, p. 175.

CLARK, JOHN and ELIZABETH HUDSON, daughter of Levin Hudson. 1799. D. B. 18, p. 390.

#CLARK, THOMAS and ELIZABETH SAMPSON, daughter of James Sampson. 1688. W. & D. B. 2, p. 291 & 386.

CLARK, THOMAS and ------- NORWOOD, sister of William Norwood. 1735. W. B. 4, p. 104.

CLARK, WILLIAM and MRS. MARY WARD, relict of Thomas Ward. 1702. W. & D. B. 2, p. 333. D. B. 2, p. 15.

CLARY, CHARLES and ELIZABETH JORDAN, daughter of Mathew Jordan. 1785. W. B. 10, p. 1. W. B. 11, p. 474.

CLARY, JAMES and MARTHA STEVENSON, daughter of Mrs. Martha Stevenson. 1773. Southampton County W. B. 3, p. 107.

CLAYTON, JOHN and MARY HOLLEMAN, daughter of Joshua J. H. Holleman. 1763. Southampton County W. B. 2, p. 136.

CLEGG, ROBERT and POLLY DOWTY, daughter of Hezekiah Dowty. 1803. O. B. 1801-3, p. 438.

CLIFTON, JOHN and LIDIA CLAUD, daughter of Joshua Claud. 1773. Southampton County W. B. 3, p. 142.

CLINCH, JOSEPH JOHN and ELIZABETH GOODRICH, daughter of George Goodrich. 1733. W. B. 3, p. 389.

COBB, EDWARD and MRS. ------- BLUNT, relict of William Blunt. 1687. W. & D. B. 2, p. 269.

COBB, GEORGE B. and ELIZABETH YOUNG. 1812. O. B. 1810-13, p. 329.

COBB, JOHN and MARY EXUM, daughter of Benjamin Exum. 1785. Southampton County W. B. 4, p. 114.

CODDIN, PHILLIP and MRS. MARY GREEN, relict of Thomas Green. 1689. D. B. I, p. 17.

COFER, JAMES and MARY SIMMONS, daughter of James Simmons. 1761. O. B. 1759-60, p. 63 & 202.

COFER, JESSE and ESTHER JONES, daughter of John Jones. 1778. W. B. 9, p. 26. W. B. 10, p. 193. D. B. 15, p. 444.

#COFER, JOHN and JANE BENNETT, daughter of Richard Bennett. 1720. G. B. 2, p. 41.

COFER, THOMAS and OLIVE WARD, daughter of Thomas Ward. 1784. D. B. 15, p. 399. W. B. 9, p. 213.

COFER, THOMAS and ELIZABETH MOODY, daughter of Phillip Moody. 1786. W. B. 10, p. 90.

COGGAN, JOHN and ------- MOORE, daughter of John Moore. 1702. W. & D. B. 2, p. 469.

COGGAN, JOHN JR. and HONOUR JOHNSON, daughter of Henry Johnson. 1794. W. B. 10, p. 308.

COGGAN, ROBERT and SARAH GREEN, daughter of John Green. 1719. G. B. 2, p. 61.

COGING, JOHN and ANN BRITT, daughter of Benjamin Britt. 1783. Southampton County W. B. 4, p. 95.

COLE, ALEXANDER and BETHIALL HILL of Salem in New England. 1688. D. B. I, p. 10.

COLLINS, JOHN and ELEANOR OLIVER, daughter of John Oliver. 1666. W. & D. B. I, p. 93.

COLLINS, WILLIAM and MRS. ANN WILDS, relict of Thomas Wilds. 1675. W. & D. B. 2, (Rev.) p. 35.

COLTER, JOHN and MRS. ------- ABBINGTON, relict of Thomas Abbington. 1693. D. B. I, (Rev.) p. 12.

COOK, JOEL and PRISCILLA ELEY, daughter of William Eley. 1761. W. B. 7, p. 144 & 468.

#COOK, REUBEN and HANNAH ATKINSON, daughter of John Atkinson. 1717. G. B. 2, p. 145. W. B. 5, p. 355.

COOK, THOMAS and MARY JONES, daughter of Arthur Jones. 1702. D. B. I, p. 383.

COOK, WILLIAM and JOANE ROPER, daughter of Hugh Roper of Somersett County, Eng. 1665. W. & D. B. I, p. 32.

COOPER, JUSINIAN and MRS. ANN HARRIS, relict of James Harris. 1628. Bk. A. p. 101. (Claimed that other extant colonial records prove this name to be Harrison.)

COPELAND, JOSEPH and MARY WOODLEY, daughter of Andrew Woodley. 1709. D. B. 2, p. 106.

COPELAND, THOMAS and HOLLAND APPLEWHAITE, daughter of Thomas Applewhaite. 1735. W. B. 4, p. 94 & 257.

CORBETT, JOHN and MRS. LUCRETIA POWELL, relict of Nathaniel Powell. 1678. W. & D. B. 2, p. 172.

CORBETT, SAMUEL and MARY NELM, daughter of John Nelms. 1785. W. B. 10, p. 6. W. B. 5, p. 293.

CORBETT, SAMUEL and MARY JOHNSON, daughter of James Johnson. 1745. W. B. 5, p. 67. W. B. 10, p. 124.

#COTTON, JOHN and MARTHA GODWIN, daughter of William Godwin. 1701. D. B. 2, p. 67. G. B. 2, p. 52.

COUNCIL, HODGES and LUCY HARDY, daughter of John Hardy. 1675. W. & D. B. 2, p. 146. D. B. 2, p. 171.

COUNCIL, JAMES and ELIZABETH BRIAND, daughter of James Briand. 1761. W. B. 7, p. 240. D. B. 12, p. 203.

COUNCIL, JOHN and MRS. ------- JEFFRIES, relict of Richard Jeffries. 1666. W. & D. B. 2, (Rev.) p. 13.

COUPLAND, JAMES and MARTHA JOHNSON, daughter of Robert Johnson.

11

1761. W. B. 7, p. 424.

COWLING, JOSIAH and URIANA MONRO, daughter of John Monro.
1769. W. B. 7, p. 22. O. B. 1768-69, p. 132.

CRESWELL, CLEMENT and MRS. ANN WHITFIELD. 1675. W. & D. B. 2,
(Rev.) p. 39.

CREW, JOHN and MOURNING SCOTT, daughter of William Scott.
1759. D. B. 10, p. 148.

CRIPPS, GEORGE and MRS. JOYCE ENGLAND, relict of Francis England.
1679. W. & D. B. 2, p. 202.

CROCKER, ANTHONY and ANN FRANCIS, daughter of John Francis.
1697. W. & D. B. 2, p. 377.

CROCKER, JOSEPH and ------- LANCASTER, daughter of Robert
Lancaster. 1760. W. B. 7, P. 53.

CROCKER, MILNER and POLLY CHAPMAN, daughter of Benjamin Chapman.
1814. W. B. 13, p. 430.

CROFT, SAMUEL and ANN BELL, sister of Benjamin Bell. 1726.
W. B. 3, p. 33.

CROOM, EDWARD and PATIENCE GARNER, daughter of James Garner.
1748. W. B. 5, p. 144. W. B. 6, p. 36.

CRUDUP, JOSHUA and MOURNING DIXON, daughter of Thomas Dixon.
1745. W. B. 5, p. 141.

CRUMP, JOHN C. and MARY WILSON, daughter of Sampson Wilson.
1810. O. B. 1810-13, p. 16.

CRUMPLER, EDMUND and MARY PEIRCE, daughter of William Peirce, Sr.
1791. W. B. 10, p.217 & 225.

CRUMPLER, WILLIAM and ELIZABETH ARRINGTON, daughter of William
Arrington. 1725. D. B. 2, p. 169. D. B. 5, p. 568.

CULLEY, CORNELIUS and MRS. ------- WRIGHT, relict of Thomas
Wright. 1667. W. & D. B. 2, p. 46 & 49.

CUNNINGHAM, JOHN and POLLY FULGHAM, daughter of Joseph Fulgham.
1782. W. B. 9, p. 303. D. B. 15, p. 44.

CUTCHIN, JOSEPH and MRS. JUDITH WILSON, relict of George Wilson.
1760. O. B. 1759-63. W. B. 6, p. 379.

CUTCHIN, JOSEPH and MRS. PRISCILLA PITT, relict of John Pitt.
1762. O. B. 1759-63, p. 298. W. B. 7, p. 61.

CUTCHINS, JOSIAH and POLLY DAVIS, daughter of John Davis.
1805. O. B. 1803-6, p. 234.

DALE, PETER and MRS. MARY MUNGER, relict of John Munger. 1675.
W. & D. B. 2, p. 102.

DANIELS, ELIAS and POLLY HOLLAND, daughter of James Holland.
1801. O. B. 1801-3, p. 125.

DANIELS, JAMES and SARAH POPE, daughter of Mrs. Priscilla Pope. 1768. W. B. 8, p. 2. D. B. 15, p. 295.

DANIELS, JOHN and MARY UZZELL, sister of James Uzzell. 1756. D. B. 9, p. 433 & 434.

DANIELS, THOMAS and ANN ALLEN, daughter of Thomas Allen. 1730. W. & D. B. 2, p. 656. D. B. 5, p. 22.

DANIELS, WILLIAM and DEBORAH GARLAND, daughter of Peter Garland. 1694. W. & D. B. 2, p. 423.

DARDEN, JACOB and -------- WILLIAMSON, daughter of George Williamson. 1721. G. B. 2, p. 118. W. B. 4, p. 77.

DARDEN, JACOB and -------- LAWRENCE, sister of Samuel Lawrence. 1739. W. B. 4, p. 332. W. B. 6, p. 246.

DARDEN, JOHN and ELIZABETH POWERS, daughter of Edward Powers Sr. 1729. W. B. 3, p. 162.

DARDEN, JOHN and -------- GILES, daughter of Hugh Giles. 1774. O. B. 1772-80, p. 254 & 281.

DARWIN, ROBERT of Ireland and ELIZABETH HILL, daughter of John Hill. 1744. D. B. 9, p. 163.

DAUGHTREY, JOHN and MARGARET LAWRENCE, daughter of John Lawrence. 1742. W. B. 5, p. 213 & 296.

DAUGHTREY, JOHN and ELIZABETH WILLIAMS, daughter of Richard Williams. 1749. Southampton County W. B. 1, p. 13. W. B. 6, p. 176 & 435.

DAUGHTREY, RICHARD and CHRISTIAN COUNCIL, daughter of Hardy Councill. 1758. D. B. 10, p. 53.

DAVIDSON, WILLIAM of Surry County and ------- CLARK, daughter of John Clark. 1721. G. B. 2, p. 124. D. B. 5, p. 397.

DAVIS, BENJAMIN and MARY MURREY, daughter of Thomas Murrey. 1740. W. B. 4, p. 315. D. B. 11, p. 62.

DAVIS, DANIEL and ELIZABETH ALLEN, daughter of Henry Allen. 1716. G. B., p. 39.

#DAVIS, EDWARD and MARTHA BRADSHAW, daughter of George Bradshaw. 1737. W. B. 5, p. 7.

DAVIS, FRANCIS and SARAH MANN, daughter of Thomas Mann. 1694. D. B. 1, p. 120.

DAVIS, JAMES and MARY HADLEY, daughter of Ambrose Hadley. 1778. W. B. 8, p. 526.

DAVIS, JOHN and MRS. MARY BRUCE, relict of John Bruce. 1666. W. & D. B. 2, (Rev.), p. 13.

DAVIS, JOHN and MARY GREEN, daughter of Thomas Green. 1686. W. & D. B. 2, p. 252 & 581.

DAVIS, JOHN and MRS. ELIZABETH LUCKS, relict of George Lucks. 1694. D. B. 1, (Rev.) p. 33.

DAVIS, JOHN and MARY GOODRICH, daughter of John Goodrich. 1746. D. B. 10, p. 248.

DAVIS, SAMPSON and ------- EDWARDS, daughter of Thomas Edwards.
1773. O. B. 1772-80, p. 129.

DAVIS, SAMUEL and AMY APPLEWHAITE, daughter of Henry Applewhaite.
1738. W. B. 4, p. 251 & 329.

DAVIS, SAMUEL and MARY MALLORY, daughter of John Mallory. 1788.
W. B. 10, p. 128 & 129.

DAVIS, THOMAS and MRS. ANN MATHEWS, relict of Anthony Mathews.
1693. D. B. I, (Rev.) p. 8. W. & D. B. 2, p. 224.

DAVIS, THOMAS and HARTWELL HODGES, daughter of Benjamin Hodges.
1752. D. B. 8, p. 455. W. B. 6, p. 47.

DAVIS, WILLIAM and MARTHA WHEADON, daughter of James Wheadon.
1760. O. B. 1759-63, p. 101.

DAW (DEW), THOMAS and ------- NICHOLDS, daughter of Thomas
Nicholds. 1680. W. & D. B. 2, p. 212.

DAWSON, DAVID and ANN EVERETT, daughter of Joseph Everett.
1773. Southampton County W. B. 3, p. 34.

DAWSON, JOHN of N. C. and MRS. ELIZABETH BODDIE, relict of John
Boddie. 1738. D. B. 5, p. 223.

DAY, JAMES and ANN ALLEN, sister of Joseph Allen. 1726.
W. B. 3, p. 15.

DAY, JAMES and MARTHA SMITH, daughter of Arthur Smith. 1742.
W. B. 4, p. 424 & 502.

DAY, JOHN and BETTY WENTWORTH, daughter of Samuel Wentworth.
1767. D. B. 15, p. 140.

DAY, THOMAS and MARY DAVIS, daughter of John Davis. 1754.
D. B. 9, p. 272. D. B. 14, (Rev.) p. 143.

DAY, THOMAS and ELIZABETH BROWN, daughter of John Brown.
(widow Fowler) 1765. Southampton County W. B. 2, p. 188.

DAY, THOMAS and ------- TYNES, daughter of Robert Tynes.
1776. W. B. 10, p. 304. O. B. 1772-80, p. 358.

#DEANS, JOHN of Nansemond County and ELIZABETH MOORE, daughter
of Isaac Moore. 1785. D. B. 15, p. 649.

DEBERRY, PETER and MARY BRANTLEY, daughter of Edward Brantley.
1712. G. B., p. 74. W. & D. B. 2, p. 554. D. B. 9,
p. 270.

DEFORD, WILLIAM and ELIZABETH CALCOTE, daughter of Harwood Calcote. 1802. O. B. 1801-3, p. 368.

DEGGE, ANTHONY and MRS. BETTY DAY, relict of John Day. 1782.
D. B. 15, p. 139.

DELOACH, MICHAEL and MOURNING POWELL, daughter of John Powell.
1760. W. B. 7, p. 140 & 141. D. B. 13, p. 495.

DELOACH, THOMAS and ------- SYKES, sister of Thomas Sykes.
1802. O. B. 1801-3, p. 152.

DENSON, JOHN and MARY BRIDELLE, daughter of Francis Bridelle.

1712. W. & D. B. 2, p. 541.

DERRING, JOHN and JANE FULGHAM, daughter of Charles Fulgham.
1812. O. B. 1810-13, p. 280.

DERRING, NICHOLAS and ANN SAMPSON, daughter of James Sampson.
1727. W. B. 3, p. 71.

DERRING, WILLIAM and ELIZABETH WILSON, daughter of George Wilson.
1792. W. B. 6, p. 379. W. B. 10, p. 226. W. B. 11,
p. 21.

DESLOGES, MICHAEL and JANE GRIFFETH, daughter of Rowland Griffeth.
1671. W. & D. B. I, p. 238.

DEWEY, GEORGE and MARY HARWOOD. Anthony Fulgham, guardian.
1666. W. & D. B. I, p. 69.

DICKINSON, CHRISTOPHER and MRS. MARY GROSS, relict of Jonathan
Gross. 1770. D. B. 12, p. 366. W. B. 9, p. 78.

DICKINSON, JACOB and MARY GOODWIN, daughter of Samuel Goodwin
(Godwin). 1755. W. B. 6, p. 247.

DICKINSON, JOEL and MARY TURNER, daughter of Joseph Turner.
1774. Southampton County W. B. 3, p. 87.

DIXON, NICHOLAS of N. C. and RACHEL BEALE, daughter of Benjamin
Beale. 1744. W. B. 4, p. 511. D. B. 8, p. 451.

DIXON, THOMAS JR. and ELIZABETH MURPHRY, daughter of Michael
Murphry. 1735. W. B. 4, p. 95. W. B. 5, p. 61.

DOBBS, JOSIAH and MARTHA BENNETT, daughter of John Bennett.
1774. D. B. 14, p. 153. O. B. 1772-80, p. 273.

DODMAN, JOHN and ELIZABETH DEATH, daughter of Richard Death.
1647. Bk. A., p. 17.

DRAKE, JOHN and MARY BROWN, daughter of Dr. Samuel Brown.
1739. W. B. 4, p. 274.

#DRAKE, THOMAS and ------- GRIFFIN, daughter of Owen Griffin.
1727. W. & D. B. 2, p. 397. W. B. 3, p. 299.

DREW, DOLPHIN and PEGGY JORDAN, daughter of Richard Jordan.
1801. O. B. 1801-3, p. 131.

DRIVER, CHARLES and PRUDENCE PITT, daughter of John Pitt.
1698. D. B. I, p. 261. W. & D. B. 2, p. 454.

DRIVER, CHARLES and ANN WHITFIELD, daughter of Mrs. Elizabeth
Whitfield. 1745. D. B. 7, p. 288.

DRIVER, EDWARD and SARAH BRAGG, daughter of James Bragg.
1727. W. B. 3, p. 82. W. B. 4, p. 111.

DRIVER, GILES and OLIVE HARDY, daughter of John Hardy. 1675.
W. & D. B. 2, p. 146.

DRIVER, GILES and PRUDENCE RICHARDS, daughter of Robert Richards.
1724. G. B. 2, p. 199. W. B. 3, p. 377.

DRIVER, JOHN and MRS. VIOLET WRIGHT, relict of George Wright.
1702. W. & D. B. 2, p. 433 & 471.

DRIVER, JOHN and SARAH HARRISON, daughter of William Harrison.
1762. W. B. 7, p. 200. O. B. 1759-63, p. 393.

DRIVER, JOHN and ------- GODWIN, sister of James Godwin.
1778. W. B. 8, p. 510.

DRUETT, JOHN and MRS. MARGARET WILLIAMSON, relict of Richard
Williamson. 1654. Bk. A, p. 85.

DUCK, JOSEPH and CHRISTIAN JOHNSON, daughter of Robert Johnson.
1787. W. B. 10, p. 89. W. B. 11, p. 28.

DUCK, WILLIAM and ELEANOR CARR, daughter of John Carr. 1734.
W. B. 4, p. 21. W. B. 7, p. 228.

DUNKLEY, JOHN and CATHERINE JOYNER, daughter of Thomas Joyner.
1740. W. B. 4, p. 267.

DUNSTON, THOMAS and SARAH SAUNDERS, daughter of Mrs. Elizabeth
Saunders. 1783. W. B. 10, p. 85 & 302.

DUPRA, JOHN and LUCY LITTLE, daughter of Robert Little. 1736.
W. B. 4, p. 136.

DURHAM, CHARLES and MRS. ------- WILLIAMS, relict of John
Williams. 1693. D. B. I, (Rev.) p. 6. W. & D. B. 2,
p. 267.

EDMUNDS, HOWELL and KERENHAPPUCK WHITFIELD, daughter of Thomas
Whitfield. 1781. W. B. 9, p. 79.

EDMUNDS, SOLOMON and ------- ENGLISH, daughter of Mrs. Mary
English. 1774. W. B. 8, p. 475.

EDWARDS, BENJAMIN and ELIZABETH DELK, sister of Shelton Delk.
1761. O. B. 1759-63, p. 63 & 449. W. B. 6, p. 72.

EDWARDS, JOHN and ------- JACKSON, daughter of John Jackson Sr.
1762. W. B. 7, p. 181.

EDWARDS, JORDAN and FANNY HARRIS, sister of John Harris. 1802.
O. B. 1801-3, p. 152.

EDWARDS, LEVY and CHARLOTTE NORSEWORTHY, daughter of Michael
Norseworthy. 1810. O. B. 1810-13, p. 6.

EDWARDS, MICHAEL and MRS. LUCY WOMBLE, relict of John Womble.
1811. O. B. 1810-13, p. 113.

EDWARDS, ROBERT and MARY HUNTT, daughter of William Huntt.
1672. W. & D. B. 2, p. 110.

EDWARDS, THOMAS and MRS. ELIZABETH PYLAND, relict of James
Pyland. 1674. W. & D. B. I, p. 328.

EDWARDS, WILLIAM and PRISCILLA WILLIAMS, daughter of Arthur
Williams. 1761. Southampton County W. B. I, p. 368.

#ELDRIDGE, SAMUEL and ------- HOOKS, sister of William Hooks.
1709. W. & D. B. 2, p. 500.

ELEY, BENJAMIN and MILLY BARKLEY, daughter of John Barkley of

Nansemond County. 1796. W. B. 10, p. 394.

ELEY, ELEY and ANN LAWRENCE, sister of Jeremiah Lawrence.
1750. W. B. 5, p. 249. W. B. 6, p. 246.

ELEY, JOHN JR. and ANN GODWIN, daughter of John Godwin. 1761.
W. B. 7, p. 97.

ELEY, MILLS and CATY LANKFORD, daughter of Stephen Lankford.
1785. W. B. 10, p. 57.

ELEY, ROBERT of Nansemond County and MARY DOUGHTIE, daughter of
John Doughtie. 1706. D. B. 2, p. 56.

ELEY, ROBERT SR. and ALICE GALE, daughter of Thomas Gale.
1732. W. B. 3, p. 331. W. B. 5, p. 276.

#ELEY, WILLIAM and ELIZABETH DENSON, daughter of William Denson.
1750. W. B. 5, p. 274.

ELSBERRY, JESSE and SARAH JONES, daughter of Thomas Jones.
1778. D. B. 14, p. 10.

ENGLISH, JESSE and MARY WATKINS, daughter of John Watkins.
1804. W. B. 12, p. 162.

ENGLISH, JOHN and REBECCA YOUNG, daughter of Bennett Young.
1812. O. B. 1810-13, p. 254.

#ENGLISH, THOMAS and ------- WATKINS, daughter of John Watkins.
1694. D. B. I, p. 183.

EVANS, WILLIAM and KATHERINE FLAKE, daughter of Robert Flake.
1689. W. & D. B. 2, p. 294. D. B. I, p. 38.

EVERETT, LEMUEL and PATSEY SMELLEY, daughter of William Smelley.
1805. O. B. 1803-6, p. 313.

EXUM, ARTHUR and MARY SIMMONS, daughter of Stephen Simmons.
1769. Southampton County O. B. 5, p. 199.

EXUM, JAMES and ANN THOMAS, daughter of Henry Thomas. 1772.
Southampton County W. B. 2, p. 460.

EXUM, JOSEPH and MRS. ELIZABETH JONES, relict of Joseph Jones.
1734. W. B. 4, p. 72. Southampton County D. B. 2, p.
173.

EXUM, ROBERT and PATIENCE WILLIAMSON, daughter of George Williamson. 1723. D. B. 5, p. 206.

EXUM, WILLIAM and PATIENCE PURSELL, daughter of Arthur Pursell.
1745. W. B. 5, p. 3. Southampton County W. B. I, p. 210.

FAWDON, GEORGE and ANN SMITH. Marriage contract. 1654.
Bk. A, p. 98(?).

FEARN, GEORGE and CATHERINE DEW, sister of William Dew of King
and Queen County. 1779. D. B. 14, p. 30.

FENERYEAR, JOHN and ANN IZARD, daughter of Richard Izard.
1669. W. & D. B. 2, p. 64.

FENN, TIMOTHY and ELIZABETH KAE, daughter of Robert Kae Sr.
1688. W. & D. B. 2, p. 289.

FIVEASH, JOHN and KAER FENN, daughter of Timothy Fenn. 1709.
W. & D. B. 2, p. 509.

#FIVEASH, PETER and MARTHA WHEADON. 1752. W. B. 6, p. 19 &
184.

FIVEASH, THOMAS and ALICE HARRIS, daughter of John Harris.
1712. W. & D. B. 2, p. 559. G. B. 2, p. 194. D. B. 7,
p. 288.

FLETCHER, JAMES and MRS. ELIZABETH JOHNSON, relict of Allen
Johnson. 1810. O. B. 1810-13, p. 45.

FORD, JOSEPH and MARY LEWIS, daughter of Daniel Lewis. 1709.
W. & D. B. 2, p. 497 & 514.

FRIZZELL, JOHN and SUSANNAH PORTIS, daughter of John Portis.
1693. D. B. I, p. 8 & 65.

FRIZZELL, RALPH and SALLY NORSEWORTHY, daughter of Tristram
Norseworthy. 1784. W. B. 9, p. 226 & 281.

FROST, JOHN and ELIZABETH DOWTY, daughter of Hezekiah Dowty.
1803. O. B. 1801-3, p. 438.

#FULGHAM, ANTHONY and REBECCA JOHNSON, daughter of Mrs. Rebecca
Johnson. 1763. W. B. 8, p. 1. W. B. 9, p. 42.

FULGHAM, CHARLES JR. and MRS. ANN WILKINSON, relict of William
Wilkinson. 1742. W. B. 4, p. 385 & 452. D. B. 11,
p. 233.

FULGHAM, CHARLES and JANE TYNES, daughter of Robert Tynes.
1790. W. B. 10, p. 304.

FULGHAM, JOHN and MARY PURSELL, daughter of Arthur Pursell.
1745. W. B. 5, p. 3 & 425.

FULGHAM, JOHN and MRS. MARY MONTGOMERY, relict of Robert Montgomery. 1761. W. B. 7, p. 76. O. B. 1764-68, p. 183.

FULGHAM, JOHN and POLLY FULGHAM, daughter of Joseph Fulgham.
1782. D. B. 15, p. 44.

FULGHAM, MICHAEL and MRS. ANN FENERYEAR, relict of John Feneryear.
1670. D. B. 9, p. 218. W. & D. B. 2, p. 64 & 307.

FULGHAM, MICHAEL and PATIENCE PITT, daughter of Henry Pitt.
1747. W. B. 5, p. 135. O. B. 1746-52, p. 81.

FULGHAM, NICHOLAS and ISABELLA HARRIS, daughter of John Harris.
1736. D. B. 8, p. 347. W. & D. B. 2, p. 559. W. B. 4,
p. 142.

FULGHAM, NICHOLAS and MRS. SARAH BRIDGER, relict of Joseph Bridger.
1760. O. B. 1759-63, p. 177. D. B. 10, p. 38.

GALE, JETHRO and ELIZABETH GARNES, daughter of John Garnes.
1761. W. B. 7, p. 184.

GALE, THOMAS and ------- MARSHALL, daughter of John Marshall.
1760. W. B. 6, p. 530. W. B. 7, p. 433.

GALE, THOMAS and FRANCES CHAPMAN, daughter of Charles Chapman.
1766. W. B. 8, p. 469. D. B. 12 p. 111.

GALE, THOMAS WHITNEY and MARY THOMAS, daughter of Richard
Thomas. 1754. D. B. 9, p. 304.

GARLAND, JOHN and ------- INNES, daughter of James Innes. 1735.
D. B. 4, p. 426. W. B. 3, p. 30.

GARLAND, PETER and JOAN WILSON, sister of William Wilson.
1655. Bk. A, p. 81. W. & D. B. 2, (Rev.) p. 10.

GASKINS, THOMAS and AMELIA POWELL, daughter of George Powell.
1801. O. B. 1801-3, p. 79.

GARTON, WILLIAM and CATHERINE RAND, daughter of William Rand Sr.
1774. O. B. 1772-80, p. 288.

GAY, JOSHUA and SARAH BABB, daughter of Mrs. Mary Babb. 1754.
W. B. 6, p. 273.

GEORGE, WILLIAM and SARAH THROPP, sister of John Thropp. 1721.
G. B. 2, p. 108.

GERUISE, THOMAS and MRS. MARY PARMENTO. Marriage Contract.
1679. W. & D. B. 2, p. 213.

GIBBS, GABRIEL and MRS. ELIZABETH WILLS, relict of Mathew Wills.
1811. O. B. 1810-13, p. 148.

GIBBS, JOHN and POLLY DRIVER, daughter of Robert Driver. 1801.
O. B. 1801-3, p. 140.

GIBBS, WILLIAM and MRS. LOIS WILLS, relict of Miles Wills.
1801. O. B. 1801-3, p. 14.

GILES, HUGH and MRS. LYDIA SUMMERELL, relict of John Summerell.
1765. W. B. 7, p. 423. W. B. 5, p. 28. O. B. 1768-69,
p. 5.

GILES, JOHN and PHILARETUS WOODWARD, daughter of Thomas Woodward.
1681. W. & D. B. 2, p. 226.

GILES, THOMAS and MRS. ELEANOR SMELLEY, relict of William Smelley.
1715. W. & D. B. 2, p. 316 & 577.

GILES, THOMAS and ------- DARDEN, daughter of Jacob Darden.
1717. W. & D. B. 2, p. 654.

#GLADHILL, REUBEN and MRS. MARY JOHNSON, relict of Dr. John
Johnson. 1712. W. & D. B. 2, p. 543 & 591.

GLOVER, JOHN and MARY PERSON, sister of Samuel Person. 1753.
W. B. 6, p. 123.

GOAD, HENRY and MRS. ------- KANEDY, relict of Morgan Kanedy.
1676. W. & D. B. 2, p. 142.

#GODWIN, BREWER and ------- FULGHAM, sister of Charles Fulgham.
1770. D. B. 12, p. 341.

GODWIN, EDMUND and ANN APPLEWHAITE, daughter of Henry Applewhaite.

19

1741. W. B. 4, p. 329. O. B. 1746-52, p. 60.

GODWIN, JAMES and SARAH KINCHIN, daughter of William Kinchin.
1734. W. B. 4, p. 72 & 113.

GODWIN, JAMES and MARTHA GODWIN, daughter of Thomas Godwin.
1749. D. B. 8, p. 308.

GODWIN, JONATHAN and CATHERINE HAWKINS, daughter of Samuel
Hawkins. 1801. O. B. 1801-3, p. 122.

GODWIN, LEMUEL and MRS. MARY RICHARDS, relict of Robert Richards.
1751. W. B. 5, p. 357. D. B. 14, (Rev.) p. 176.

#GODWIN, MATHEW of Nansemond County and CHARLOTTE DURLEY,
daughter of Mrs. Mary Durley. 1759. W. B. 10, p. 49.
D. B. 11, p. 48.

GODWIN, ROBERT and JANE LYNTH, daughter of Francis Lynth.
1664. W. & D. B. I, p. 28.

GODWIN, THOMAS and ELIZABETH, granddaughter of Richard Wilkinson. 1741. W. B. 4, p. 418.

GODWIN, THOMAS and MARY MOSCROP, daughter of Thomas Moscrop.
1745. W. B. 5, p. 14. O. B. 1746-52, p. 310.

GODWIN, WILLIAM and ELIZABETH WRIGHT, daughter of Thomas Wright.
1666. W. & D. B. I, p. 79.

#GODWIN, WILLIAM and ANN PITT, daughter of John Pitt. 1729.
W. B. 4, p. 43.

GODWIN, WILLIAM and MARTHA BUNKLEY, daughter of Joshua Bunkley.
1801. O. B. 1801-3, p. 145.

GOLDHAM, HENRY and MRS. MARY BECHINOE, relict of Edward Bechinoe.
1706. D. B. 2, p. 51.

GOLDHAM, THOMAS and MRS. ELIZABETH DANIELS, relict of John
Daniels. 1679. W. & D. B. 2, (Rev.) p. 49.

GOLDSBOROUGH, NICHOLAS of Tablott County, Maryland and ANN
POWELL, daughter of Thomas Powell. 1695. D. B. I,
p. 195.

GOODRICH, EDWARD and JULIANA DAVIS, daughter of John Davis.
1754. D. B. 9, p. 272. W. B. 6, p. 508.

GOODRICH, JOHN and MARGARET BRIDGER, daughter of Joseph Bridger.
1751. W. B. 5, p. 373.

GOODSON, EDWARD and MARY THOMAS, daughter of Phillip Thomas.
1702. W. & D. B. 2, p. 456.

#GOODSON, EDWARD and MARY MANDEW, daughter of Thomas Mandew of
Bartie County, N. C. 1737. D. B. 5, p. 152.

#GOODSON, GEORGE and SARAH MANDEW, daughter of Thomas Mandew of
Bartie County, N. C. 1737. D. B. 5, p. 152.

GOODSON, JOHN and MARTHA FULGHAM, daughter of Charles Fulgham.
1812. O. B. 1810-13, p. 280.

GRANTHAM, EDWARD and MRS. ------- COCKEN, relict of William

20

Cocken. 1678. W. & D. B. 2, (Rev.) p. 45.

GRAY, HENRY and SARAH HARDING, daughter of Mrs. Sarah Harding. 1747. W. B. 5, p. 261.

GRAY, JOSIAH and MARTHA WILLS, daughter of Miles Wills. 1796. W. B. 11, p. 135.

GREEN, GEORGE and ANN EXUM, daughter of Jeremiah Exum. 1705. W. & D. B. 2, p. 475.

GREEN, PETER and PATIENCE RICHARDS, daughter of Robert Richards. 1733. W. B. 3, p. 377.

GREEN, THOMAS and MARY MOON, daughter of Thomas Moon. 1694. D. B. 1, p. 154.

GREEN, THOMAS and MARY SELLOWAY, daughter of John Selloway. 1745. D. B. 7, p. 224.

GREEN, WILLIAM and MARY WEST, daughter of William West. 1708. W. & D. B. 2, p. 490. W. B. 3, p. 182.

GREEN, WILLIAM and ------- WAILE, daughter of Nicholas Waile. 1798. W. B. 11, p. 122. O. B. 1801-3, p. 359.

GRIFFIN, EDWARD and MARY MUMFORD, niece of Thomas Mumford. 1698. D. B. 1, p. 271.

GRIFFIN, MATHEW and KATHERINE JONES, daughter of Thomas Jones Sr. 1748. W. B. 5, p. 238. Southampton County W. B. 1, p. 41.

GRIFFIN, MICHAEL and LUCY JONES, daughter of Brittain Jones. 1776. D. B. 13, p. 389.

GRIFFIN, SHADRACH and ------- NELMS, daughter of John Nelms. 1785. W. B. 10, p. 6.

GRIFFIN, THOMAS and ANNE WRIGHT, daughter of Thomas Wright. 1666. W. & D. B. 1, p. 85.

GRIFFETH (GRIFFIN), OWEN and MRS. MARY EDWARDS, relict of Robert Edwards. 1694. D. B. 1, (Rev.) p. 57. W. & D. B. 2, p. 397.

GROSS, FRANCIS and MRS. MARY BEVAN, relict of Thomas Bevan. 1744. D. B. 7, p. 24.

GROSS, JONATHAN and MARY NORSEWORTHY, daughter of Joseph Norseworthy. 1757. W. B. 6, p. 315. O. B. 1759-63, p. 330 & 504.

GROSS, RICHARD and JANE WILSON, daughter of John Wilson. 1669. W. & D. B. 1, p. 209.

GROVE, GEORGE and MRS. MARY BECHINOE, relict of George Bechinoe. 1687. W. & D. B. 2, p. 275 & 321.

GROVE, WILLIAM and MRS. ELEANOR CARTER, relict of Thomas Carter. 1673. W. & D. B. 2, p. 120 & 172. W. & D. B. 1, p. 317.

GWALTNEY, JOSEPH and ANN SIMMONS, daughter of James Simmons. 1762. O. B. 1759-63, p. 380.

GWALTNEY, WILLIAM and ELIZABETH WOMBWELL, daughter of Thomas Wombwell. 1784. W. B. 9, p. 294.

GWILLIAM, HINCHA and ------- WEST, sister of Francis West. 1715. W. & D. B. 2, p. 631.

HADLEY, AMBROSE and MARTHA CROCKER, daughter of Edward Crocker. 1751. W. B. 5, p. 442. W. B. 8, p. 526.

HAILE, JOHN and HANNAH MORRIS, daughter of John Morris. 1772. W. B. 8, p. 197.

HAILE, WILLIAM and TABITHA THOMAS, daughter of Richard Thomas. 1761. W. B. 7, p. 132 & 188.

HALL, ISAAC and MARY NORSEWORTHY, daughter of Tristram Norseworthy. W. B. 9, p. 226.

HALL, JOHN and CHRISTAIN POOLE, daughter of Thomas Poole. 1681. W. & D. B. 2, p. 228.

HALL, THOMAS and ELIZABETH PITT, daughter of Joseph Pitt. 1769. O. B. 1768-69, p. 98.

#HAMPTON, JOHN and ANN NEVELLE, daughter of Roger Nevelle. 1718. G. B., p. 190.

HAMPTON, THOMAS and ELIZABETH BRIDLE, daughter of Francis Bridle. 1689. D. B. 1, p. 23.

HANSON, CHARLES and MRS. SOPHIA RAND, relict of William Rand. 1778. O. B. 1772-80, p. 439.

HARDIMAN, THOMAS and MRS. LUCRETIA TOMLIN, relict of Joseph Tomlin. 1757. D. B. 14, (Rev.) p. 180.

HARDY, GEORGE and MARY JACKSON, daughter of Richard Jackson. 1666. W. & D. B. 1, p. 76.

HARDY, RICHARD and MARY CHAMBERS, daughter of William Chambers. 1742. D. B. 6, p. 105.

HARDY, THOMAS and MARTHA ATKINSON, daughter of William Atkinson. 1804. O. B. 1803-6, p. 109.

HAREBOTTLE, THOMAS and MRS. REBECCA GOODRICH, relict of John Goodrich Sr. 1704. W. & D. B. 2, p. 389 & 467.

HARGRAVE, JESSE and ------- PERSON, sister of Samuel Person. 1753. W. B. 6, p. 123.

HARRIS, EDWARD and MARY THORPE, daughter of Timothy Thorpe. 1739. W. B. 4, p. 293. Southampton County W. B. 1, p. 37.

HARRIS, JOHN and MARGARET HOBBS, sister of Francis Hobbs. 1687. W. & D. B. 2, p. 280.

HARRIS, JOHN and MARY DREW, daughter of Edward Drew. 1745. Southampton County W. B. 1, p. 8.

HARRIS, LEWIS and SARAH THORPE, daughter of John Thorpe. 1771.

Southampton County W. B. 2, p. 457.

HARRIS, LEWIS and MARY POWELL. 1804. O. B. 1803-6, p. 46.

HARRIS, THOMAS and ------- EDWARDS, daughter of Robert Edwards.
1758. D. B. 10, p. 51.

HARRIS, THOMAS and SARAH LANE, daughter of Richard Lane. 1760.
Southampton County D. B. 3, p. 6.

HARRISON, HENRY and ------- NORWOOD, sister of William Norwood.
1735. W. B. 4, p. 103.

HARRISON, JOHN and MILBORAN BRESSIE, sister of William Bressie.
1699. W. & D. B. 2, p. 431. D. B. 2, p. 151.

#HARRISON, JOHN and ANN NOYALL, daughter of William Noyall.
1746. W. B. 5, p. 41 & 189.

HARRISON, JOHN and ELIZABETH HILL, daughter of Francis Hill.
1788. W. B. 10, p. 210.

HARRISON, WILLIAM and MARY HODGES, daughter of Ellis Hodges.
1755. D. B. 9, p. 344.

HART, ARTHUR of North Carolina and MARTHA WARREN, daughter of
Thomas Warren. 1750. Southampton County D. B. 1, p. 81.

HART, HARDY of North Carolina and JANE WARREN, daughter of
Thomas Warren. 1750. Southampton County D. B. 1, p. 81.

HARVEY, JOHN and DOROTHY TOOK, daughter of James Took. 1659.
W. & D. B. 1, p. 590.

HARVEY, JOHN and MRS. PRUDENCE WILLS, relict of John Wills Jr.
1774. O. B. 1772-80, p. 314. W. B. 9, p. 15.

#HATCHELL, WILLIAM and CHRISTIAN MORRIS, daughter of John Morris.
1760. W. B. 8, p. 197. D. B. 10, p. 239.

HATTON, LEWIS of Norfolk County and ELIZABETH GOODRICH, daughter
of Edward Goodrich. 1774. D. B. 13, p. 210.

HAWKINS, THOMAS and MARY MACONE, daughter of Neal Macone. 1680.
W. & D. B. 2, p. 214 & 346.

HAYES, THOMAS and ELIZABETH FLAKE, daughter of Robert Flake.
1697. D. B. 5, p. 140. G. B., p. 511.

HAYNES, WILLIAM and JULIANA BREWER, daughter of Thomas Brewer.
1761. Southampton County D. B. 3, p. 94.

HAYNES, WILLIAM and CATHERINE BAKER, daughter of Lawrence Baker.
1766. W. B. 7, p. 10 & 452. W. B. 11, p. 723.

HAYWOOD, WILLIAM and SARAH THOMAS. 1756. D. B. 9, p. 416.

HEATH, ROBERT and ROSEY DOWTY, daughter of Hezekiah Dowty.
1803. O. B. 1801-3, p. 438.

HERBERT, JOHN MARKHAM of Norfolk County and JANE SUMMERELL,
daughter of John Summerell. 1765. O. B. 1764-68,
p. 224. W. B. 5, p. 28.

HILL, HENRY of North Carolina and MARY HILL, daughter of Joseph

Hill. 1764. D. B. 11, p. 227.

HILL, JOSEPH and LUCY MILLER, daughter of Mrs. Lucy Miller.
1778. W. B. 9, p. 118.

HILL, NICHOLAS and SILVESTRA BENNETT, daughter of Edward Bennett.
1675. W. & D. B. 2, p. 133.

#HILL, THOMAS and MARY MARSHALL, daughter of Humphry Marshall.
1711. W. & D. B. 2, p. 533.

HOBBS, FRANCIS SR. and MRS. MARY FLOYD, relict of Nathan Floyd.
1674. W. & D. B. 1, p. 323.

HODGES, BENJAMIN and MRS. ------- HARRISON, relict of John
Harrison. 1732. W. B. 3, p. 318.

HODGES, JOHN JR. and COMFORT CARY, daughter of Mrs. Patience
Cary. 1766. D. B. 12, p. 65.

HODGES, JOHN and MRS. MARY MILLER, relict of John Miller.
1779. O. B. 1772-80, p. 466. D. B. 15, p. 561.

HODGES, ROBERT and ANN BRANCH, daughter of George Branch. 1725.
G. B., p. 721.

HODSDEN, WILLIAM and OLIVE SMITH, daughter of Arthur Smith.
1742. W. B. 4, p. 424. W. B. 6, p. 419.

HODSDEN, WILLIAM and SARAH BRIDGER, daughter of Joseph Bridger.
1797. W. B. 11, p. 19. D. B. 18, p. 157.

HOLE, JOHN and MARY SMITH, daughter of Arthur Smith. 1688.
W. & D. B. 2, p. 288 & 377.

HOLLAND, JOB and MARY DAUGHTRY, daughter of John Daughtry Sr.
1783. W. B. 9, p. 247. W. B. 10, p. 172.

HOLLIDAY, ANTHONY and MRS. ANN BREWER, relict of John Brewer.
1671. W. & D. B. 2, p. 100. D. B. 1, p. 16.

HOLLIDAY, ANTHONY and EASTER WILKINSON, daughter of Richard
Wilkinson. 1741. W. B. 4, p. 418.

HOLLIDAY, JOSEPH and POLLY W. GALE, daughter of Thomas Gale.
1809. D. B. 21, p. 73.

HOLLIDAY, JOSIAH and ------- SMITH, daughter of Joseph Smith.
1782. O. B. 1780-83, p. 57.

HOLLIMAN, ARTHUR and CATY BRITT, daughter of Edward Britt Sr.
1789. Southampton County W. B. 4, p. 372.

HOLLIMAN, ARTHUR and SALLY APPLEWHAITE. 1812. O. B. 1810-13,
p. 246.

#HOLLIMAN, JESSE and CHARITY COFER, daughter of Thomas Cofer.
1783. W. B. 9, p. 213.

HOLLOWELL, JOSEPH and ------- WILLIAMS, daughter of John Williams.
1754. W. B. 6, p. 131.

HOLLOWELL, WILLIAM and SARAH SCOTT, daughter of Thomas Scott.
1764. O. B. 1764-68, p. 71. W. B. 9, p. 104.

24

HOLT, THOMAS and ANN JONES, daughter of Mathew Jones. 1744.
     D. B. 6, p. 500.

HOOKS, ROBERT and MRS. MARY POWELL, relict of Stephen Powell.
     1693. G. B., p. 560. D. B. 1, p. 66.

HORSEFIELD, STEPHEN and REBECCA THORNTON, daughter of Mrs.
     Kath. Thornton. 1673. W. & D. B. 1, p. 216. W. & D.
     B. 2, p. 271.

HOUGHLOW, WILLIAM and MARY PARKER, daughter of Thomas Parker.
     1788. W. B. 10, p. 111. W. B. 11, p. 309.

HOUSE, JOSHUA and ELIZABETH EVERETT, daughter of Joseph Everett.
     1756. W. B. 6, p. 290.

HOUSE, ROBERT JR. and MARTHA SPILTIMBER, daughter of Anthony
     Spiltimber. 1704. D. B. 1, p. 419.

HOWARD, JOHN and MRS. JANE DAVIS, relict of John Davis. 1764.
     O. B. 1764-68, p. 109. W. B. 7, p. 145.

HOWELL, JOHN and ELIZABETH SURBEY, daughter of John Surbey.
     1731. D. B. 4, p. 154.

HOWELL, MATHEW and MARY LANE, daughter of Joseph Lane. 1719.
     G. B. 2, p. 26.

HUGHES, JOHN of Norfolk County and PHILARITA GILES, daughter
     of Hugh Giles. 1773. D. B. 13, p. 35.

#HUNT, GODFREY of Nansemond County and MARGARET GODWIN, daughter
     of Edmund Godwin. 1719. G. B., p. 250.

HUTCHIN, FRANCIS JR. and ELIZABETH COBB, Guardian, Pharoah Cobb.
     1679. W. & D. B. 2, p. 192.

HUTCHINS, FRANCIS and SARAH POWELL, daughter of John Powell.
     1730. W. B. 3, p. 257. D. B. 5, p. 303.

HUTCHINS, RICHARD of Nansemond County and ELIZABETH COBB,
     daughter of Joseph Cobb Jr. 1693. D. B. 1, p. 85.

#INGLES, THOMAS and ELIANOR WATKINS, daughter of John Watkins.
     1688. D. B. 1, p. 15.

INGRAM, WILLIAM and SARAH ATKINSON, daughter of James Atkinson.
     1737. W. B. 4, p. 241. Southampton County W. B. 1,
     p. 243.

INMAN, JOHN and SARAH DAWSON, daughter of Martin Dawson. 1745.
     W. B. 5, p. 51 & 73.

JACKSON, RICHARD and ------- BENNETT, daughter of Mrs. Alice
     Bennett. 1647. Bk. A, p. 4. W. & D. B. 1, p. 69.

JAMES, JOHN and PATIENCE BOOTH, daughter of Shelly Booth.
     1771. Southampton County W. B. 2, p. 435.

JARRELL, THOMAS and MARTHA KINCHIN, daughter of William Kinchin.
1734. W. B. 4, p. 72 & 113.

JARRETT, CHARLES and MRS. MARY HARDY, relict of Thomas Hardy.
1717. W. & D. B. 2, p. 622 & 625.

JENKINS, VALENTINE and MRS. SALLY CHAPMAN, relict of Hardy
Chapman. 1812. O. B. 1810-13, p.238.

JENNINGS, JOHN and MARTHA HARRIS, daughter of Robert Harris.
1668. W. & D. B. 1, p. 128.

JENNINGS, JOHN and MRS. MARY SEWARD, relict of William Seward.
1678. W. & D. B. 2, p. 173.

JENNINGS, JOHN and MARY HILL, daughter of Nicholas Hill. 1695.
D. B. 1, p. 202. D. B. 2, p. 148.

JOHNSON, ABRAHAM and ANN JONES, daughter of Thomas Jones Sr.
1748. W. B. 5, p. 238.

JOHNSON, BENJAMIN and PRUDENCE DRIVER, daughter of Giles Driver.
1751. D. B. 8, p. 418.

JOHNSON, BENJAMIN and ------- NELMS, daughter of John Nelms.
1785. W. B. 10, p. 6.

JOHNSON, JAMES and MARY JOHNSON, daughter of Robert Johnson.
1692. D. B. 1, p. 49.

JOHNSON, JAMES and MRS. SARAH HAINES, relict of Edward Haines.
1759. D. B. 10, p. 132.

JOHNSON, JESSE and MARY ATKINSON, daughter of Samuel Atkinson.
1785. Southampton County W. B. 4, p. 115.

JOHNSON, JOHN and MRS. MARY DAY, relict of James Day. 1703.
W. & D. B. 2, p. 484 & 543.

JOHNSON, ROBERT and MARTHA JONES, daughter of Thomas Jones Sr.
1737. D. B. 5, p. 172. W. B. 5, p. 238.

JOHNSON, SAMUEL and MARY DRIVER, daughter of Giles Driver.
1751. D. B. 8, p. 418.

JOHNSON, WILLIAM and ------- GRIFFETH, daughter of Owen Griffeth.
1698. W. & D. B. 2, p. 397.

JOHNSTON, JAMES and ELIZABETH SMITH, daughter of Thomas Smith.
1799. W. B. 11, p. 211.

JOHNSTON, DR. ROBERT and MARY PONSONBY, daughter of William
Ponsonby. 1762. W. B. 7, p. 66. D. B. 11, p. 61.

JONES, ARTHUR and SUSANNAH KING, daughter of Henry King.
1679. W. & D. B. 2, p. 192 & 565.

JONES, DAVID and CELIA CASEY, daughter of Nicholas Casey.
1764. W. B. 7, p. 244. O. B. 1764-68, p. 302.

JONES, EDWARD and DEBORAH EXUM, daughter of William Exum.
1700. W. & D. B. 2, p. 436. W. B. 3, p. 210.

JONES, ELBERTON and ELIZABETH SIMMONS, daughter of John Simmons.
1746. Southampton County W. B. 1, p. 8.

JONES, FRANCIS and MARY RIDLEY, daughter of Nathaniel Ridley.
1750. W. B. 5, p. 322.

JONES, JAMES and MRS. ELIZABETH WRENCH, relict of John Wrench.
1760. W. B. 7, p. 4.

JONES, JOHN and MRS. ELIZABETH WOLLARD, relict of Henry Wollard.
1668. W. & D. B. 2, p. 69.

JONES, JOHN and ELINOR DAWSON, daughter of Martin Dawson.
1745. W. B. 5, p. 51.

JONES, JOHN and ANN YOUNG, daughter of Bennett Young. 1812.
O. B. 1810-13, p. 254.

JONES, JONATHAN and ELIZABETH BROWN, daughter of Robert Brown.
1763. W. B. 7, p. 351.

JONES, JOSEPH and ELIZABETH KINCHIN, sister of William Kinchin.
1726. W. B. 3, p. 43. W. B. 4, p. 113.

JONES, JOSEPH and MRS. AMY DAVIS, relict of Samuel Davis.
1746. W. B. 5, p. 97 & 211.

JONES, JOSEPH and MARTHA BRIDGER, daughter of Joseph Bridger.
1751. W. B. 5, p. 373.

JONES, LEMUEL and KATHERINE LAWRENCE, daughter of John Lawrence.
1776. W. B. 8, p. 151. O. B. 1772-80, p. 339.

JONES, MATHEW and MRS. ELIZABETH RIDLEY, relict of Nathaniel
Ridley. 1723. G. B. 2, p. 151.

JONES, MATHEW and ------- WILLIAMS, daughter of Mrs. Mary
Williams. 1734. W. B. 4, p. 28.

JONES, NATHANIEL and MRS. MARY HURST, relict of John Hurst.
1739. W. B. 3, p. 58. D. B. 5, p. 445.

#JONES, SAMUEL and PATIENCE JORDAN, daughter of John Jordan.
1781. W. B. 9, p. 74. D. B. 12, p. 474.

JONES, THOMAS and MRS. PATIENCE WHITEHEAD, relict of Arthur
Whitehead Jr. 1750. W. B. 5, p. 172 & 288.

JONES, WILLIAM and MRS. MARY ARMOUR, relict of William Armour.
1694. D. B. 1, (Rev.) p. 52.

JONES, WILLIS and CELIA BOYCE, daughter of William Boyce. 1794.
W. B. 10, p. 324.

#JORDAN, ARTHUR of North Carolina and ELIZABETH TURNER, daughter
of James Turner. 1750. D. B. 8, p. 367.

JORDAN, BILLINGSLEY and ------- GOODWIN, daughter of Samuel
Goodwin (Godwin). 1770. D. B. 12, p. 355.

JORDAN, GEORGE of North Carolina and PATIENCE WARREN, daughter
of Thomas Warren. 1759. Southampton County D. B. 2,
p. 331.

JORDAN, JAMES and PATIENCE TERRELL, daughter of Blackaby Terrell.
1726. W. B. 3, p. 360.

JORDAN, JAMES and PATIENCE JORDAN, daughter of Richard Jordan.

1746. D. B. 9, p. 180.

JORDAN, JOHN and MARTHA HARDING, daughter of Mrs. Sarah Harding.
1747. W. B. 5, p. 261.

JORDAN, JOSEPH and PATIENCE RICKS, daughter of Abraham Ricks.
1746. W. B. 5, p. 26 & 32.

JORDAN, JOSEPH and WILMOUTH WILLIAMSON, daughter of Burwell
Williamson. 1792. Southampton County W. B. 4, p. 531.

JORDAN, JOSHUA and ELIZABETH SANBORNE, daughter of Daniel
Sanbourne. 1711. W. & D. B. 2, p. 546.

JORDAN, JOSIAH and MOURNING RICKS, daughter of Abraham Ricks.
1746. W. B. 5, p. 26 & 32.

JORDAN, MATHEW and MRS. SUSANNAH BRESSIE, relict of William
Bressie. 1713. D. B. 1, p. 347.

JORDAN, MATHEW and SUSANNAH BIRD, daughter of Robert Bird.
1724. G. B., p. 648.

JORDAN, MATHEW and MARY BRACEY, daughter of Mrs. Elizabeth
Bracey. 1751. W. B. 5, p. 456.

JORDAN, PLEASANTS and ELIZABETH FULGHAM, daughter of Charles
Fulgham. 1812. O. B. 1810-13, p. 280.

JORDAN, RICHARD and ELIZABETH REYNOLDS, daughter of Christopher
Reynolds. 1654. Bk. A, p. 46. W. & D. B. 2, p. 62.

JORDAN, RICHARD and REBECCA RATCLIFF, daughter of Richard Ratcliff. 1713. W. & D. B. 2, p. 638.

JORDAN, ROBERT and CHRISTIAN TABERER, daughter of Thomas Taberer.
1695. D. B. 1, p. 223.

JORDAN, WILLIAM and MARY EXUM, sister of Francis Exum. 1753.
Southampton County W. B. 1, p. 127. D. B. 14, (Rev.)
p. 122.

JOYNER, JOSEPH and ELIZABETH SMELLEY, daughter of Lewis Smelley.
1722. G. B., p. 488.

JOYNER, THEOPHILUS and HENRIETTA GRIFFIN, daughter of Andrew
Griffin. 1724. W. B. 4, p. 255. Southampton County
W. B. 1, p. 139.

JOYNER, THOMAS and MARGARET MORRISON, daughter of William
Morrison. 1802. W. B. 11, p. 722.

JOYNER, WILLIAM and MRS. ANN ELEY, relict of Eley Eley. 1750.
W. B. 5, p. 249. W. B. 6, p. 246.

KAE, ROBERT and MRS. ANNE GOODRICH, relict of John Goodrich.
1697. D. B. 1, p. 246.

KEEBLE, TOBIAS and MRS. ------- LEWIS, relict of Arthur Lewis.
1671. W. & D. B. 2, p. 99.

KINCHEN, WILLIAM and ELIZABETH JOYNER, daughter of Thomas

Joyner. 1735. W. B. 4, p. 73 & 113. W. & D. B. 2, p. 486.

KING, HENRY and KATHERINE CLARKE, daughter of John Clarke of Surry County. 1684. Surry County (Small) D. B. 2, p. 13.

KING, HENRY and MARTHA BROWNE, daughter of Dr. Samuel Browne. 1740. W. B. 4, p. 274.

KING, JOHN and MRS. FANNY WHITFIELD, relict of Samuel Whitfield. 1805. O. B. 1803-6, p. 417.

KING, THOMAS and ------- TYNES, daughter of Robert Tynes. 1790. W. B. 10, p. 304.

KIRLE, WILLIAM and ELLIANOR MURFREY, daughter of William Murfrey. 1710. D. B. 2, p. 162.

KIRLE, WILLIAM and MARGARET COBB, daughter of Robert Cobb. 1710. G. B. 2, p. 58.

KNOTT, JAMES and MARY HOLLIDAY, daughter of Anthony Holliday. 1718. W. & D. B. 2, p. 644.

LAMBETH, JOHN and MARY RICHARDSON, daughter of William Richardson. 1764. O. B. 1764-68, p. 281 & 394.

LANE, JOSEPH of Sussex County and ELIZABETH GWALTNEY, daughter of William Gwaltney. 1780. D. B. 14, p. 138.

LANE, TIMOTHY and ------- SHAW, daughter of Mrs. Elizabeth Shaw. 1752. W. B. 6, p. 28.

LANKFORD, THOMAS and MRS. MARGARET DAUGHTRY, relict of John Daughtry. 1773. D. B. 13, p. 123.

LARIMORE, ROGER and MRS. ANN GADSBIE, relict of Richard Gadsbie. 1678. W. & D. B. 2, p. 176.

LAWRENCE, JOHN and MARGARET MURFREY, daughter of William Murfrey. 1717. G. B. 2, p. 88. W. B. 5, p. 296.

LAWRENCE, JOHN and MARTHA RICKS, daughter of Abraham Ricks. 1746. W. B. 5, p. 26 & 32.

LAWRENCE, JOHN and ------- TYNES, daughter of Thomas Tynes. 1769. W. B. 8, p. 69.

LAWRENCE, JOSIAH and MRS. SALLY FRIZZELL, relict of Ralph Frizzell. 1803. O. B. 1801-3, p. 464.

LAWRENCE, ROBERT and MRS. ------- GAY, relict of Henry Gay. 1689. D. B. 1, p. 16. G. B. 2, p. 59.

LAWRENCE, ROBERT and SARAH EXUM, daughter of Jeremiah Exum. 1719. D. B. 2, p. 291. W. B. 3, p. 19.

LAWRENCE, ROBERT and ANNE COUNCIL, daughter of Hardy Council. 1743. W. B. 4, p. 522.

LAWRENCE, ROBERT and SARAH ELEY, daughter of Robert Eley Sr.

1795. W. B. 10, p. 363.

LAWRENCE, WILLIAM and PENELOPE BROWNE, daughter of Dr. Samuel
Browne. 1739. W. B. 4, p. 274.

LAWRENCE, WILLIAM and SARAH APPLEWHAITE, daughter of Mrs. Ann
Applewhaite. 1746. W. B. 5, p. 97. W. B. 6, p. 269.

LEAR, JOHN and MRS. ANN GEORGE, relict of John George. 1681.
W. & D. B. 1, p. 460.

LEAR, THOMAS and ELIZABETH BRIDGER, daughter of Joseph Bridger.
1686. W. & D. B. 2, p. 255.

LEE, JOHN and ELIZABETH MURREY, daughter of Thomas Murrey.
1740. W. B. 4, p. 315.

LESTER, ANDREW and MRS. SARAH COUNCIL, relict of Lemuel Council.
1802. O. B. 1801-3, p. 331.

LEWIS, FIGUERS and PATSEY DRIVER, daughter of Mrs. Prudence
Driver. 1801. O. B. 1801-3, p. 140.

LEWIS, JOHN and MRS. ANN MACONE, relict of Neale Macone. 1690.
W. & D. B. 2, p. 214 & 304.

LEWIS, MORGAN and SARAH GEORGE, daughter of John George. 1678.
W. & D. B. 2, p. 148 & 170.

LEWIS, THOMAS and REBECCA GEORGE, daughter of John George.
1678. W. & D. B. 2, p. 88 & 156.

LIGHTFOOT, BARTHOLOMEW and SARAH GODWIN, daughter of Lemuel
Godwin. 1767. D. B. 12, p. 167.

LIGHTFOOT, THOMAS and MRS. SARAH JORDAN, relict of Joshua Jordan.
1749. O. B. 1746-52, p. 222.

LILE, THOMAS and MRS. KATHERINE GILES, relict of Hugh Giles.
1761. O. B. 1759-63, p. 206.

LITTFORD, JOHN and MRS. ------- DAYLEY, relict of Peter Dayley.
1668. W. & D. B. 2, p. 56.

LITTLE, JOHN and ------- JACKSON, daughter of John Jackson Sr.
1762. W. B. 7, p. 181.

LITTLE, WILLIAM and FRANCES LITTLE, daughter of Francis Little.
1716. G. B. 2, p. 9.

#LONG, ROBERT and SUSANNAH GROSS, daughter of Thomas Gross.
1715. W. & D. B. 2, p. 645 & 660.

LOVETT, THOMAS and MARY HOWELL, sister of Hopkins Howell.
1708. D. B. 2, p. 113.

LOWRY, MATHEW and MRS. JOANA GOODSON FLOYD, daughter of Edward
Goodson. 1735. G. B. 2, p. 127. W. B. 4, p. 86.

LUCKS, JOHN and MRS. SARAH JENNINGS INGRAM, sister of John
Jennings. 1695. W. & D. B. 2, p. 408. G. B., p. 646.

LUCKS, JOHN and MARTHA FULGHAM, daughter of Nicholas Fulgham.
1710, G. B. 2, p. 170. W. & D. B. 2, p. 514.

LUCKS, JOHN and ------- CLARK, daughter of John Clark. 1759.
 W. B. 6, p. 518. O. B. 1759-63, p. 148.

LUKE, PAUL and MRS. MARY LLEWELLEN, relict of Thomas Llewellen.
 1664. W. & D. B. 1, p. 26.

#LUNDY, RICHARD and MARY SMITH, daughter of Thomas Smith.
 1740. W. B. 4, p. 334.

LUTER, JOHN and MARY BEAL, daughter of Benjamin Beale. 1680.
 D. B. 1, p. 322. D. B. 8, p. 353.

LUPO, JAMES and SARAH BRANCH, daughter of George Branch of
 Surry County. 1679. D. B. 1, p. 4. W. & D. B. 2,
 p. 202 & 285.

LUPO, JAMES and ANN ATKINSON, daughter of Benjamin Atkinson.
 1786. D. B. 15, p. 704. W. B. 10, p. 347.

LUPO, PHILLIP and MILDRED CARRELL, daughter of William Carrell.
 1785. W. B. 9, p. 298. W. B. 10, p. 198.

MACKEY, ADAM and MARY STREET, daughter of George Street. 1756.
 D. B. 9, p. 419. W. B. 3, p. 334.

MACKEY, WILLIAM and REBECCA MARKS, daughter of Thomas Marks.
 1771. Southampton County W. B. 2, p. 466.

MACKINNIE, BARNABY and MRS. MARY MURFREY, relict of William
 Murfrey. 1719. G. B. 2, p. 19.

MACKLEMORE, JOHN and ELIZABETH SPENCE, daughter of William
 Spence. 1750. Southampton County D. B. 1, p. 215 & 266.

MACODDIN, PHILLIP and MRS. MARY GREEN, relict of Thomas Green.
 1693. D. B. 1, (Rev.) p. 7.

MADDERA, ZACHARIAS and PRISCILLA DEBERRY, daughter of Peter
 Deberry. 1712. W. & D. B. 2, p. 554.

MADDERY, JAMES and MARY WOMBWELL, daughter of Thomas Wombwell.
 1784. W. B. 9, p. 294.

MADDERY, JOSEPH and MARGARET WOMBWELL, daughter of Thomas
 Wombwell. 1784. W. B. 9, p. 294.

MALLORY, JOHN and MARY DAVIS, daughter of John Davis. 1754.
 D. B. 9, p. 272. D. B. 14, (Rev.) p. 143.

MARSHALL, HUMPHREY and MRS. ANN SMITH, relict of Nicholas Smith.
 1696. D. B. 1, p. 214.

#MARSHALL, JAMES and MARY HAMPTON, daughter of Thomas Hampton.
 1747. W. & D. B. 2, p. 459. W. B. 5, p. 79.

MARSHALL, JOHN and ANN RICKS, daughter of Abraham Ricks.
 1746. W. B. 5, p. 26 & 32.

MARSHALL, ROBERT and MARY PENNY, daughter of Richard Penny.
 1693. W. & D. B. 2, p. 344.

MARTIN, HENRY and MRS. MARY DIXSON, relict of Thomas Dixson.

1670. W. & D. B. 2, p. 91.

MASON, LITTLEBERRY and REBECCA BLUNT, daughter of William Blunt.
1787. Southampton County W. B. 4, p. 232.

MATHEWS, HUGH and MARTHA JOHNSON, daughter of John Johnson.
1715. G. B., p. 271. W. & D. B. 2, p. 484.

MATHEWS, SAMUEL and SARAH GARNES, daughter of John Garnes.
1761. W. B. 7, p. 184.

MAYO, WILLIAM and ISABEL HARDY, daughter of John Hardy. 1681.
W. & D. B. 1, p. 459.

MAZRY, ROBERT and SUSANNA DODMAN, daughter of John Dodman.
1679. W. & D. B. 1, p. 429.

MEACOM, LEWIS and ANN WRENN, daughter of Mrs. Mary Wrenn.
1745. W. B. 5, p. 2 & 62.

MEADOR, BANISTER and MRS. POLLY BENN YOUNG, relict of Bennett
Young. 1812. O. B. 1810-13, p. 254.

MECONE, WILLIAM and SARAH GARLAND, daughter of Peter Garland.
1694. W. & D. B. 2, p. 423.

MERCER, THOMAS and MRS. MARTHA CHESTNUTT, relict of John Chestnutt. 1750. O. B. 1746-52, p. 332. D. B. 9, p. 437.

MEREDITH, JOSEPH and SARAH DENSON, daughter of Francis Denson.
1708. W. & D. B. 2, p. 496.

MIAL, THOMAS and SARAH BROWN, daughter of Thomas Brown. 1765.
Southampton County W. B. 2, p. 112.

MIDDLETON, OWEN of Surry County and ELEAN BROWNE. Marriage
Contract. 1669. W. & D. B. 1, p. 215.

#MILLER, JOHN and ALICE BELL, daughter of John Bell. 1721.
G. B. 2, p. 113.

MILLER, NICHOLAS and ------- CASEY, daughter of Thomas Casey.
1758. D. B. 10, p. 58.

MILLER, THOMAS and REBECCA CLAYTON, daughter of John Clayton.
1756. W. B. 6, p. 458.

MILLER, THOMAS and MRS. MARY RICHARDS, relict of Robert Richards.
1758. D. B. 10, p. 63.

MINGTON, JEPTHA and ------- TYNES, daughter of Thomas Tynes.
1769. W. B. 8, p. 69.

MINTON, ELIAS and ------- BULLARD, daughter of Thomas Bullard.
1772. W. B. 8, p. 125.

MINTZ, EDWARD and ANN BRADDY, daughter of Mason Braddy. 1785.
W. B. 9, p. 334.

MIRICK, OWEN and MARY THROPE, daughter of Timothy Thrope.
1750. Southampton County W. B. 1, p. 37.

MITCHELL, JAMES of Nansemond County and ELIZABETH PITT, sister
of John Pitt. 1783. D. B. 15, p. 308.

32

MONRO, REV. ANDREW and MRS. SARAH PITT, daughter of Arthur
Smith. 1697. W. & D. B. 2, p. 377 & 544.

MONRO, JOHN of Nansemond County and ELIZABETH NORSEWORTHY,
daughter of George Norseworthy. 1738. W. B. 4, p. 221.

MOODY, ISAAC and ------- BLUNT, daughter of William Blunt.
1780. W. B. 9, p. 45. O. B. 1780, p. 1.

MOONE, THOMAS and MRS. PRUDENCE WILSON. 1655. Bk. A, p. 81.
W. & D. B. 2, (Rev.) p. 7.

MOORE, GEORGE and JANE BARECROFT, daughter of Charles Barecroft.
1661. W. & D. B. 2, (Rev.) p. 1.

MOORE, JOHN and ANN GILES, daughter of John Giles. 1739.
D. B. 5, p. 358.

MOORE, THOMAS and MRS. ------- ELDRIDGE, relict of Samuel
Eldridge. 1667. W. & D. B. 2, p. 49. (Rev.) p. 10.

MOORE, THOMAS and SARAH WAINWRIGHT, daughter of William Wainwright. 1762. O. B. 1759-63, p. 331.

MORRIS, JESSE and ELIZABETH LIGHTFOOT, daughter of Lemuel Lightfoot. 1805. O. B. 1803-6, p. 236.

#MORRISON, JAMES and SARAH DRIVER, daughter of Charles Driver.
1784. W. B. 9, p. 266.

MUNGER, JOHN and MRS. MARY BUSHELL, relict of Edward Bushell
of Surry County. 1669. W. & D. B. 2, p. 71.

MURPHRY, MICHAEL and ------- HAMPTON, sister of John Hampton.
1735. W. B. 4, p. 95. W. B. 5, p. 61 & 79.

MURPHRY, WILLIAM and SARAH HOLLIDAY, daughter of Anthony Holliday. 1718. W. & D. B. 2, p. 644. G. B. 2, p. 88.

MURREY, ALEXANDER and MRS. ANN COLLINS, relict of William Collins. 1687. W. & D. B. 2, (Rev.) p. 62.

MURREY, JOHN and ELIZABETH YARRETT, daughter of William Yarrett.
1679. W. & D. B. 2, p. 229.

MURREY, JOHN and MRS. MARY PARMENTO, relict of John Parmento.
1715. W. & D. B. 2, p. 597.

MURREY, JOHN and MRS. ANN GLOVER, relict of William Glover.
1762. O. B. 1759-63, p. 285. W. B. 6, p. 422.

MURREY, RALPH and MRS. ALEXANDERA KAE, relict of Robert Kae.
1724. G. B. 2, p. 161.

MURREY, ROBERT and ------- MOSCROP, daughter of Thomas Moscrop.
1745. W. B. 5, p. 14.

MURREY, THOMAS and SARAH DAVIS, sister of John Davis. 1740.
W. B. 4, p. 315. O. B. 1746-52, p. 229.

MURREY, WILLIAM and MARY DAVIS, daughter of John Davis. 1712.
W. & D. B. 2, p. 581.

NELMS, JEREMIAH and NANCY GWALTNEY, daughter of Patrick Gwaltney.
1805. O. B. 1803-6, p. 422.

NELMS, JOHN and MRS. ELIZABETH MACKMIAL, relict of John Mackmial.
1750. W. B. 5, p. 293. W. B. 10, p. 6.

NELSON, WILLIAM of Surry County and ANN BAKER, daughter of
Lawrence Baker. 1766. W. B. 7, p. 10 & 452. W. B.
11, p. 723.

NELSON, WILLIAM and MRS. MARTHA WILKINSON, relict of Willis
Wilkinson. 1804. O. B. 1803-6, p. 86.

#NEVILL, JOHN and ELIZABETH REYNOLDS, sister of Richard Reynolds.
1689. D. B. 1, p. 25.

#NEWMAN, JAMES and ELINOR WRENCH, daughter of John Wrench.
1782. W. B. 9, p. 172 & 239.

NEWMAN, JOHN and RUTH TABERER, daughter of Thomas Taberer.
1692. W. & D. B. 2, p. 350.

NEWMAN, JOHN and ------- EVERETT, daughter of William Everett.
1770. W. B. 8, p. 44.

NEWMAN, THOMAS and MARY RATCLIFF, daughter of Richard Ratcliff.
1713. W. & D. B. 2, p. 638.

NEWMAN, THOMAS and MRS. MARY BUNKLEY, relict of Robert Bunkley.
1727. W. B. 3, p. 57. W. B. 4, p. 295.

NIBLETT, EDWARD and SALLY HOUGH, sister of John Hough. 1802.
O. B. 1801-3, p. 152.

NIBLETT, JOHN of Charles City County and MARY WASHBORNE, daughter
of Daniel Washborne. 1673. W. & D. B. 1, p. 288.

NOLLIBOY, DANIEL and SARAH TARLETON, daughter of Roger Tarleton.
1726. W. B. 3, p. 161. D. B. 10, p. 136.

NORSEWORTHY, GEORGE and MARTHA PITT, daughter of John Pitt.
1702. W. & D. B. 2, p. 454. D. B. 2, p. 59.

NORSEWORTHY, GEORGE and ------- WEBB, daughter of James Webb.
1717. W. & D. B. 2, p. 619. G. B. 2, p. 173 & 182.

NORSEWORTHY, GEORGE and CHRISTIAN EXUM, daughter of Jeremiah
Exum. 1719. W. B. 3, p. 19. D. B. 2, p. 291.

NORSEWORTHY, GEORGE and MRS. RACHEL PARKER, relict of Thomas
Parker. 1742. W. B. 4, p. 418 & 511.

NORSEWORTHY, JOHN and FRANCES ENGLISH, daughter of John English.
1670. W. & D. B. 2, p. 82, 166 & 310.

NORSEWORTHY, JOSEPH and MARY BRAGG, daughter of James Bragg.
1729. W. B. 3, p. 82. W. B. 4, p. 111.

NORSEWORTHY, TRISTRAM and SARAH PITT, daughter of John Pitt.
1702. W. & D. B. 2, p. 454. G. B. 2, p. 167.

NORSEWORTHY, TRISTRAM and EASTER BAGNALL, daughter of Nathan
Bagnall. 1754. W. B. 6, p. 130. D. B. 14, p. 26.

NORSEWORTHY, TRISTRAM and HONOUR GOODRICH, daughter of John

Goodrich. 1759. O. B. 1759-63, p. 14. W. B. 5, p. 191.

NORSEWORTHY, TRISTRAM of Nansemond County and MRS. ------- SMITH, relict of Nicholas Smith. 1768. D. B. 12, p. 233.

OAKS, JOSEPH and ELIZABETH LITTLE, daughter of Robert Little. 1736. W. B. 4, p. 136.

OGBURNE, NICHOLAS and ANN SMITH, daughter of Mrs. Mary Smith. 1713. G. B. 2, p. 37. W. B. 4, p. 286.

OUTLAND, JOHN and ELIZABETH BRACEY, daughter of Mrs. Elizabeth Bracey. 1751. W. B. 5, p. 456.

OUTLAND, JOHN and SARAH BABB, sister of William Babb. 1796. W. B. 11, p. 11.

OUTLAND, WILIAM and JANE EXUM, daughter of Jeremiah Exum. 1719. D. B. 2, p. 291. W. B. 3, p. 19.

OUTLAND, WILLIAM of Nansemond County and ANN SCOTT, daughter of James Took Scott. 1762. D. B. 11, p. 101.

PAINE, ANTHONY and PEGGY OUTLAND, daughter of John Outland. 1798. W. B. 11, p. 104 & 146.

PALMER, EDMOND and MRS. ------- DUNSTON, relict of Robert Dunston. 1680. W. & D. B. 1, p. 420.

PARDOE, PHILLIP and MRS. REBECCA LEWIS, relict of Thomas Lewis. 1678. W. & D. B. 2, p. 89 & 156.

PARKER, FRANCIS and ELIZABETH SMITH, daughter of William Smith. 1705. W. & D. B. 2, p. 470, 605 & 628.

PARKER, FREDERICK and MRS. MARY DRIVER, relict of Giles Driver. 1764. O. B. 1764-68, p. 274 & 483.

PARKER, RICHARD and MRS. JUDITH HUNTT, relict of William Huntt. 1668. W. & D. B. 2, p. 51 & 77.

PARKER, RICHARD and SARAH JARRELL, daughter of Thomas Jarrell. 1741. W. B. 4, p. 391.

PARKER, THOMAS and RACHEL WILKINSON, daughter of Richard Wilkinson. 1741. W. B. 5, p. 511.

PARKER, WILLIAM and MARY ROBERTS, daughter of John Roberts. 1711. W. & D. B. 2, p. 567.

PARKER, WILLIAM and ANN APPLEWHAITE, daughter of Mrs. Martha Applewhaite. 1739. W. B. 4, p. 257.

PARKER, WILLIAM and MARY BEAL, daughter of Benjamin Beal. 1780. W. B. 9, p. 143. W. B. 10, p. 39.

PARKERSON, HENRY and REBECCA LITTLE, daughter of John Little. 1792. W. B. 10, p. 242.

PARKETT, EDWARD and MARGARET TYNES, daughter of Nicholas Tynes.
1708. W. & D. B. 2, p. 489.

PARNELL, JOHN and MRS. ------- CHESTNUTT, relict of Alexander
Chestnutt. 1690. W. & D. B. 2, (Rev.) p. 75.

PARR, THOMAS and ELIZABETH JORDAN, daughter of Richard Jordan.
1739. D. B. 7, p. 531.

PARTRIDGE, JAMES and FRANCES PENNY, daughter of Richard Penny.
1693. D. B. 1, p. 182. W. & D. B. 2, p. 344.

#PASS, WILLIAM and MRS. SARAH BURK, relict of John Burk. 1767.
O. B. 1764-68, p. 489.

PASTEUR, JOHN and HONOUR WILSON, daughter of George Wilson.
1792. W. B. 6, p. 379. W. B. 10, p. 226.

PATTERSON, WILLIAM and MRS. FRANCES GIBBS, relict of Gabriel
Gibbs. 1798. W. B. 11, p. 99.

PEDIN, JAMES and MRS. JANE HUGGENS, relict of Mathew Huggens.
1672. W. & D. B. 2, p. 88. (Rev.) p. 31.

PEDIN, JAMES and MARY WILKINSON, daughter of Richard Wilkinson.
1741. W. B. 4, p. 418.

PENNY, JOHN and MARY MARSHALL, sister of Humphrey Marshall.
1735. W. B. 4, p. 90 & 524.

PERKINS, WILLIAM and MRS. SARAH LAWRENCE, relict of George
Lawrence. 1810. O. B. 1810-13, p. 1.

PERRY, JOHN and ELIZABETH YOUNG, daughter of John Young.
1674. W. & D. B. 2, (Rev.) p. 34.

PERRY, JOSEPH and MRS. ELIZABETH LUNDY, relict of James Lundy Sr.
1717. G. B. 2, p. 153. W. B. 3, p. 253.

PERRY, WILLIAM and MRS. MARY VALENTINE, relict of James Valentine.
1679. W. & D. B. 2, p. 192.

PERSON, JACOB and MARY ATKINSON, daughter of Joseph Atkinson.
1761. W. B. 7, p. 390. D. B. 12, p. 201.

PERSON, JOHN and PRUDENCE JONES, daughter of Samuel Jones.
1770. W. B. 8, p. 74.

PERSON, JOSEPH and ANN JONES, daughter of Samuel Jones.
1770. W. B. 8, p. 74.

#PEUGH, DAVID and ELIZABETH WHITFIELD, daughter of Abraham
Whitfield. 1787. W. B. 10, p. 81 & 82.

PHILLIPS, JOHN and ------- CLARK, daughter of John Clark.
1721. G. B. 2, p. 124. D. B. 5, p. 397.

PIERCE, JOHN and MRS. ------- BROWN, relict of John Brown.
1666. W. & D. B. 2, p. 43.

PIERCE, JOHN and ESTHER HUTCHENS, daughter of Richard Hutchens.
1735. D. B. 4, p. 439.

PIERCE, THOMAS and MRS. KATHERINE EVANS, relict of William Evans.
1691. D. B. 1, p. 38.

PIERCE, THOMAS and STRATFIELD THROPP, daughter of Thomas Thropp.
1720. G. B. 2, p. 108. D. B. 9, p. 261.

PIERCE, THOMAS and MRS. HONOUR WILSON, relict of James Wilson.
1742. W. B. 4, p. 408 & 456.

PIERCE, THOMAS and MARTHA DIXON, daughter of Thomas Dixon.
1746. W. B. 5, p. 141.

PIERCE, THOMAS and MARY WENTWORTH, daughter of Samuel Wentworth.
1767. D. B. 15, p. 140.

PILAND, JAMES and MRS. ELIZABETH GREENWOOD, relict of Thomas
Greenwood. 1674. W. & D. B. 1, p. 328.

#PILAND, JAMES and COMFORT CARRELL, daughter of William Carrell.
1785. W. B. 9, p. 298.

PILAND, RICHARD and ELINOR MOORE, daughter of George Moore.
1714. W. & D. B. 2, p. 194 & 586.

PINHORN, JOHN and COURTNEY SCOTT, daughter of Thomas Scott.
1782. D. B. 15, p. 78.

PINNER, DIXON and NANCY DRIVER, daughter of Robert Driver.
1800. W. B. 11, p. 485.

PITMAN, THOMAS and ELIZABETH LANCASTER, daughter of Robert
Lancaster. 1720. G. B. 2, p. 28.

PITT, HENRY and MRS. ANN WATSON, relict of Robert Watson.
1655. Bk. A, p. 29 & 68.

PITT, HENRY and MARY BAGNALL, daughter of Nathan Bagnall.
1754. W. B. 6, p. 130 & 282.

PITT, HENRY and ELIZABETH GODWIN, daughter of Edmond Godwin.
1762. W. B. 7, p. 175. O. B. 1759-63, p. 360.

#PITT, HENRY and JULIANA BAGNALL, daughter of Richard Bagnall.
1773. W. B. 8, p. 241. O. B. 1772-80, p. 388(?).

PITT, JAMES and PATIENCE GODWIN, daughter of Joseph Godwin.
1757. W. B. 7, p. 50.

PITT, JAMES and MRS. MARY SMITH, relict of Joseph Smith.
1779. O. B. 1772-80, p. 490.

PITT, JAMES and SALLY SHIVERS, daughter of William Shivers Sr.
1805. O. B. 1803-6, p. 314.

PITT, JOHN and MRS. OLIVE BROMFIELD, relict of John Bromfield.
1702. W. & D. B. 2, p. 454.

#PITT, JOHN and ------- GODWIN, sister of Thomas Godwin.
1748. W. B. 5, p. 164.

PITT, ROBERT and MARY BRIDGER, daughter of Joseph Bridger.
1760. O. B. 1759-63, p. 177 & 207.

PITT, THOMAS and MRS. MARY HOLE, relict of John Hole. 1696.
W. & D. B. 2, p. 288 & 377.

PITT, THOMAS and MARY BULLOCK, daughter of Joseph Bullock.
1777. W. B. 9, p. 40.

37

PITT, WILLIS and ELIZABETH NORSEWORTHY, daughter of Tristram
    Norseworthy. 1784. W. B. 9, p. 226.

PLEASANTS, JOHN and ------- JORDAN, daughter of Josiah Jordan.
    1786. W. B. 10, p. 30.

PONSONBY, WILLIAM and CATY VELLINES, daughter of Twaite Vellines.
    1768. W. B. 11, p. 106. D. B. 12, p. 251.

POOLE, JOSEPH and MRS. ELIZABETH CHAMPION. 1668. W. & D. B. 2,
    p. 65.

POOLE, RICHARD and MRS. MARY DAVIS, relict of John Davis.
    1665. W. & D. B. 1, p. 67.

POPE, HENRY and SARAH WATTS, daughter of John Watts. 1697.
    W. & D. B. 2, p. 386.

POPE, JOHN and ELIZABETH POWELL, daughter of William Powell.
    1695. D. B. 1, p. 193.

POPE, JOHN and SWEETING PARNALL, daughter of James Parnall.
    1769. D. B. 12, p. 301. W. B. 8, p. 17.

POPE, NATHAN and ------- WILLIAMS, daughter of John Williams.
    1754. W. B. 6, p. 131.

POPE, RICHARD and ANN WILLIAMS, daughter of John Williams.
    1754. W. B. 6, p. 131.

POPE, RICHARD and CATHERINE SAUNDERS, daughter of Robert
    Saunders. 1792. W. B. 10, p. 270.

PORTLOCK, CHARLES and LYDIA RIDLEY, daughter of Nathaniel
    Ridley. 1750. W. B. 5, p. 322.

POTTER, JOHN and MRS. ANN MEACOM, relict of Lewis Meacom.
    1745. W. B. 5, p. 2 & 62.

POWELL, BENJAMIN and REBECCA GODWIN, daughter of Kinchin Godwin.
    1806. O. B. 1803-6, p. 504.

POWELL, JAMES and MRS. ANN PITT, relict of Henry Pitt. 1667.
    W. & D. B. 1, p. 115.

POWELL, JOHN of Nansemond County and DEBORAH HERN, daughter of
    Henry Hern. 1700. D. B. 1, p. 337.

POWELL, JOSHUA and MARY TOMLIN, daughter of Mrs. Martha Tomlin.
    1789. W. B. 10, p. 243.

POWELL, STEPHEN and MRS. MARY BOAZMAN, relict of Ralph Boazman.
    1723. G. B., p. 560.

POWELL, THOMAS and ------- SMITH, daughter of Nicholas Smith.
    1695. D. B. 1, p. 195.

POWELL, THOMAS and MRS. MARY TOMLIN, relict of John Tomlin.
    1767. O. B. 1764-68, p. 470.

PRETLOW, JOHN and MARY BRACEY, daughter of Mrs. Elizabeth
    Bracey. 1765. W. B. 8, p. 47.

PRICE, JOSEPH and MARTHA WILLIAMSON, daughter of Francis Wil-
    liamson. 1725. W. B. 3, p. 133.

PRICE, THOMAS and RACHEL HERN, daughter of Henry Hern. 1700.
D. B. 1, p. 320.

PRICE, WILLIAM and ELIZABETH GODWIN, daughter of Edmond Godwin
of Nansemond County. 1721. G. B., p. 448.

PRITCHARD, THOMAS and ELIZABETH RICKS, daughter of Abraham
Ricks. 1746. W. B. 5, p. 26 & 32.

PROCTOR, JEREMY and BRIDGET GREEN, daughter of Thomas Green.
1706. W. & D. B. 2, p. 252 & 475.

PROCTOR, REUBEN and MRS. JOAN BURNETT, relict of Robert Burnett.
1710. G. B. 2, p. 118. Surry County Bk. 5, p. 33.

PROCTOR, REUBEN and MRS. SARAH WARD, relict of Benjamin Ward.
1758. D. B. 9, p. 528. W. B. 5, p. 417.

PRUDEN, JOHN and MOURNING WATKINS, daughter of John Watkins.
1804. W. B. 12, p. 162.

PULLEN, ABRAHAM and MRS. MARIABLE NICHOLSON, relict of Richard
Nicholson. 1673. W. & D. B. 2, p. 118.

#PURDIE, GEORGE and FRANCES WENTWORTH, daughter of Samuel
Wentworth. 1768. W. B. 7, p. 511. O. B. 1772-80, p. 284.

PURDIE, THOMAS and SARAH TYNES, daughter of Robert Tynes.
1802. O. B. 1801-3, p. 356. O. B. 1810-13, p. 235.

RAND, WILLIAM and SOPHIA ALLMAND, daughter of James Allmand.
1757. W. B. 6, p. 306. O. B. 1759-63, p. 176.

RANDOLPH, ROBERT and MRS. ANN POWELL, relict of James Powell.
1693. D. B. 1, (Rev.) p. 12.

RAWLINS, ROGER of Surry County and ELIZABETH SKINNER, daughter
of Richard Skinner. 1677. W. & D. B. 2, p. 152.
D. B. 2, p. 45.

REEVES, THOMAS OF North Carolina and MRS. ELIZABETH MACKQUINNEY,
relict of Michael Mackquinney. 1701. D. B. 1, p. 339.

#REGAN, FRANCIS of Surry County and JANE GROSS, daughter of
Richard Gross. 1696. D. B. 1, p. 226. G. B., p. 534.

REYLEY, EDWARD and MRS. ------- CRUDOPP, relict of Barnard
Crudopp. 1679. W. & D. B. 2, p. 192.

REYNOLDS, CHRISTOPHER and ELIZABETH SAUNDERS, sister of John
Saunders. 1747. O. B. 1746-52, p. 29.

REYNOLDS, CHRISTOPHER and MARY LIGHTFOOT, daughter of Henry
Lightfoot. 1753. W. B. 6, p. 122. D. B. 9, p. 154.

REYNOLDS, CHRISTOPHER and MRS. PENELOPE NOLLIBOY, relict of
Needham Nolliboy. 1763. O. B. 1759-63, p. 464.

REYNOLDS, GEORGE and ELIZABETH NORSEWORTHY, daughter of Joseph
Norseworthy. 1757. W. B. 6, p. 315. O. B. 1759-63,
p. 330 & 504.

#REYNOLDS, MICHAEL of North Carolina and ALICE DARDEN, daughter of Joseph Darden. 1737. D. B. 5, p. 157. D. B. 8, p. 268.

REYNOLDS, RICHARD and ELIZABETH WILLIAMS, daughter of George Williams. 1685. W. & D. B. 2, p. 243. D. B. 1, p. 90.

REYNOLDS, RICHARD and ------- STAPLES, daughter of Richard Staples. 1690. D. B. 8, p. 242. D. B. 1, p. 25.

REYNOLDS, RICHARD and ------- SHARPE, daughter of Richard Sharpe. 1699. W. & D. B. 2, p. 422.

REYNOLDS, ROBERT and PATIENCE LIGHTFOOT, daughter of Henry Lightfoot. 1754. W. B. 6, p. 122. D. B. 9, p. 289.

REYNOLDS, ROWLAND and ------- CHAPMAN, daughter of Joseph Chapman. 1791. W. B. 10, p. 220.

REYNOLDS, SHARPE and SOPHIA GODWIN, daughter of Samuel Godwin. 1784. W. B. 9, p. 230. W. B. 10, p. 205.

RICHARDS, JOHN and MRS. ANN MADDISON, relict of Richard Maddison. 1678. W. & D. B. 1, p. 375.

RICHARDS, ROBERT and MRS. MARTHA LUCKS, relict of John Lucks. 1715. W. & D. B. 2, p. 514 & 595. G. B. 2, p. 170.

RICHARDS, ROBERT and MRS. MARY GOODWIN, relict of Lemuel Goodwin (Godwin). 1758. D. B. 10, p. 63. D. B. 14, (Rev.), p. 176.

RICHARDS, THOMAS and MRS. ANN OGBURNE, relict of Nicholas Obburne. 1713. W. & D. B. 2, p. 629. W. B. 4, p. 286.

RICHARDS, WILLIAM and MRS. FRANCES BENN, relict of Arthur Benn. 1732. W. B. 3, p. 314.

RICHARDS, WILLIAM and MRS. MARTHA WILLS, relict of Thomas Wills. 1754. W. B. 6, p. 101. W. B. 7, p. 95 & 504.

RIDDICK, GEORGE and MRS. ANN KAE, relict of Capt. Robert Kae. 1710. W. & D. B. 2, p. 509.

RIDDICK, JAMES and MRS. ------- SHEPHERD, relict of John Shepherd. 1689. W. & D. B. 2, (Rev.) p. 72.

RIDLEY, JAMES and JANE SMITH, daughter of Arthur Smith. 1742. W. B. 4, p. 424. D. B. 7, p. 53.

RIDLEY, NATHANIEL and ELIZABETH DAY, daughter of James Day. 1706. W. & D. B. 2, p. 475.

RIDLEY, NATHANIEL and PRISCILLA APPLEWHAITE, daughter of Henry Applewhaite. 1742. W. B. 4, p. 329. Southampton County W. B. 1, p. 120.

ROBERTS, BARDEN and ELIZABETH EVERETT, daughter of John Everett. 1811. O. B. 1810-13, p. 141.

ROBERTS, JOHN and JANE BRASWELL, sister of Richard Braswell. 1680. W. & D. B. 2, p. 567.

ROBERTS, THOMAS and MRS. ELIZABETH BRAGG, relict of James Bragg. 1674. W. & D. B. 2, p. 124.

ROBERTSON, WILLIAM and MARY APPLEWHAITE, daughter of Thomas
    Applewhaite. 1770. W. B. 8, p. 64. D. B. 12, p. 466.

ROGERS, JOHN and MARY BOOTH, sister of Richard Booth. 1681.
    W. & D. B. 1, p. 473.

RONALD, ANDREW and MARY FRY, daughter of Mrs. Mary Fry. 1783.
    W. B. 10, p. 309.

RONALDSON, PATRICK and MRS. MARY EASSON, relict of James Easson.
    1769. W. B. 9, p. 16. W. B. 10, p. 212.

#ROOKINGS, WILLIAM of Surry County and ELLEN WILLIAMS, daughter
    of Jones Williams. 1740. D. B. 5, p. 523.

ROTCHELL, GEORGE and MARY BOYKIN. 1751. Southampton County
    D. B. 1, p. 246.

RUFFIN, BENJAMIN and LUCY SIMMONS, daughter of John Simmons.
    1746. Southampton County W. B. 1, p. 8.

RUFFIN, EDWARD and ANN SIMMONS, daughter of John Simmons.
    1746. Southampton County W. B. 1, p. 8.

RUTTER, WALTER and MARTHA IZARD, daughter of Richard Izard.
    1686. D. B. 1, p. 240.

SAMFORD, THOMAS and FRANCES AMIS, daughter of James Amis of
    Gloucester County. 1761. D. B. 10, p. 310.

SAMPSON, JAMES and ELIZABETH BARECROFT, daughter of Charles
    Barecroft. 1666. W. & D. B. 1, p. 84.

SANDERS, HENRY and MARGARET SELLAWAY, daughter of John Sellaway.
    1712. G. B. 2, p. 158.

SANDERSON, JONATHAN and FRANCES SEAGRAVE, daughter of Francis
    Seagrave. 1725. W. B. 3, p. 56.

SANDIFUR, WILLIAM and MARY TOMKINS, daughter of Samuel Tomkins.
    1762. Southampton County D. B. 3, p. 131.

SAVAGE, JOEL and REBECCA WARD, daughter of Thomas Ward. 1783.
    O. B. 1780-83, p. 187.

SAWYER, THOMAS and ISABELL FRIZZELL, daughter of William Friz-
    zell. 1706. W. & D. B. 2, p. 479.

SCAMMELL, JOHN of North Carolina and HENRIETTA CUTCHINS, sister
    of Joseph Cutchins. 1750. D. B. 8, p. 307. W. B. 7,
    p. 327.

SCOTT, JAMES TOOK and CHRISTIAN NORSEWORTHY, daughter of George
    Norseworthy. 1739. W. B. 4, p. 351 & 375.

SCOTT, JOHN and SARAH CLIFTON, daughter of Thomas Clifton.
    1755. Southampton County D. B. 2, p. 54.

SCOTT, JOSEPH and ANN LAWRENCE, daughter of John Lawrence.
    1776. W. B. 8, p. 151. O. B. 1772-80, p. 339.

SCOTT, ROBERT and JANE ROBERTS, daughter of John Roberts.

1711. W. & D. B. 2, p. 530 & 567.

SCOTT, THOMAS and ------- MURRY, sister of Thomas Murry. 1798.
W. B. 11, p. 115.

SCOTT, WILLIAM and ELIZABETH WHITE, daughter of John White.
1718. W. & D. B. 2, p. 649.

SCOTT, WILLIAM and MOURNING EXUM, daughter of Jeremiah Exum.
1719. D. B. 2, p. 291. W. B. 3, p. 19.

SCOTT, WILLIAM and ELIZABETH RICKS, daughter of Robert Ricks.
1745. D. B. 7, p. 271.

SELDEN, BARTHOLOMEW of Nansemond County and ------- ASHLEY,
granddaughter of Christopher Ashley. 1718. G. B.,
p. 184.

SELLAWAY, JOHN and JANE RICKS, daughter of Isaac Ricks.
1730. D. B. 4, p. 96.

SHELLEY, PHILLIP of Surry County and SARAH WAKEFIELD, daughter
of John Wakefield. 1700. D. B. 1, p. 314.

SHEPHERD, SAMUEL and MRS. PRUDENCE HARRISON, relict of Richard
Harrison. 1810. O. B. 1810-13, p. 44.

SHIPLEY, JONATHAN of Bridge Town in the Barbadoes and ELLIS
BURNELL, daughter of John Burnell. 1681. D. B. 1, p. 23.

SHIVERS, JONAS and PATIENCE DIXON, daughter of Thomas Dixon.
1746. W. B. 5, p. 141.

SHIVERS, JOSEPH and MRS. MARY HOWELL, relict of Thomas Howell.
1782. O. B. 1780-83, p. 64.

SHIVERS, JOSEPH and CHLOE NEWMAN, sister of Josiah Newman.
1801. W. B. 11, p. 774.

SHUMACKE, ARNOLD and MRS. ANN WILLIAMS, relict of John Williams.
1694. D. B. 1, p. 107.

SIKES, ANDREW and CHLOE HOUGH, sister of John Hough. 1802.
O. B. 1801-3, p. 152.

SIKES, THOMAS and MRS. ELIZABETH HAMPTON, relict of Thomas
Hampton. 1708. W. & D. B. 2, p. 491.

SIKES, THOMAS and ELIZABETH GALE, daughter of Thomas Gale.
1730. W. B. 3, p. 254 & 332.

SIMMONS, CHARLES and ELEANOR BUTTS, daughter of Thomas Butts
of New Kent County. 1753. Southampton County D. B.
1, p. 504.

SIMMONS, CHARLES and MARY WAINWRIGHT, daughter of William Wainwright. 1761. O. B. 1759-63, p. 269.

SIMMS, JOHN of Brunswick County and MRS. HONOUR LIGHTFOOT,
sister of Thomas Pierce. 1754. D. B. 9, p. 261.
D. B. 14, (Rev.) p. 94.

SIMS, CHARLES of North Carolina and ESTHER MURRY, daughter of
Thomas Murry. 1762. D. B. 11, p. 62.

SINCLAIR, JOHN and ANN WILSON, daughter of George Wilson. 1792. W. B. 6, p. 379. W. B. 10, p. 226. W. B. 11, p. 21.

SINCLAIR, JOHN and MRS. MARY J'ANSON, relict of Thomas J'Anson. 1801. O. B. 1801-3, p. 107.

SKINNER, ARTHUR and MRS. ------- NEVILLE, relict of William Neville. 1665. W. & D. B. 1, p. 48.

#SMELLEY, JOHN and SARAH CASEY, daughter of Richard Casey. 1745. W. B. 5, p. 112. W. B. 7, p. 369.

SMELLEY, JOHN and MARY RICHARDS. 1762. W. B. 7, p. 173.

SMELLEY, LEWIS and ELIZABETH GILES, daughter of Thomas Giles. 1710. D. B. 2, p. 169.

SMELLEY, ROBERT and ELLENOR GILES, daughter of Thomas Giles. 1715. W. & D. B. 2, p. 597.

SMELLEY, THOMAS and FANNY CHAPMAN, daughter of John Chapman. 1769. W. B. 8, p. 3.

SMELLEY, WILLIAM and BETSEY PINNER, daughter of John Pinner. 1776. W. B. 10, p. 9.

SMITH, ARTHUR and SARAH JACKSON, daughter of Richard Jackson. 1666. W. & D. B. 1, p. 69.

SMITH, ARTHUR and MARY BROMFIELD, daughter of John Bromfield. 1734. D. B. 4, p. 397.

SMITH, JAMES and MARY CHAPMAN, daughter of Joseph Chapman. 1805. O. B. 1803-6, p. ·277.

SMITH, JOHN and ANN STREET, sister of Maddison Street. 1732. W. B. 3, p. 335.

SMITH, JOHN and ------- SHAW, daughter of Mrs. Elizabeth Shaw. 1752. W. B. 6, p. 28.

SMITH, JOSEPH and MARY RAND, daughter of William Rand Sr. 1774. O. B. 1772-80, p. 288.

SMITH, ROBERT and ------- BATTEN, daughter of Daniel Batten. 1678. W. & D. B. 2, p. 164 & 459.

SMITH, WILLIAM and MRS. ANN DOWNES, relict of John Downes. 1693. D. B. 1, (Rev.) p. 24.

SMITH, WILLIAM and ELIZABETH GODWIN, daughter of Joseph Godwin. 1757. W. B. 7, p. 50. W. B. 8, p. 56.

SMITH, WILLIAM and ANN COVINGTON HOLLIDAY, daughter of Samuel Holliday. 1760. O. B. 1759-63, p. 144 & 342.

SMITH, WILLIAM and MRS. ELIZABETH BROCK, relict of Benjamin Brock. 1764. O. B. 1764-68, p. 294.

SNOWDEN, RICHARD and MARGARET BROWN, daughter of Robert Brown. 1746. W. B. 5, p. 22. W. B. 7, p. 351.

SOJURNOUR, JOHN and MRS. ALICE HARRIS. Marriage Contract. 1673. W. & D. B. 2, p. 124.

SPILTIMBER, ANTHONY and MARY HARRIS, daughter of Robert Harris. 1668. W. & D. B. 1, p. 128.

SPYVIE, BENJAMIN and LUCY ROSE, sister of William Rose. 1771. W. B. 8, p. 113.

STALLINGS, JOHN and ELIZABETH WARD, daughter of Joseph Ward. 1762. W. B. 7, p. 428 & 513. W. B. 10, p. 94.

STANTLIN, DARBY and MRS. JULIANA KING. 1670. W. & D. B. 2, p. 90.

STANTON, JAMES and ANN NEWBY, daughter of Thomas Newby. 1801. O. B. 1801-3, p. 124. W. B. 11, p. 91.

STEVENS, BENJAMIN and MRS. MARY SELLAWAY, relict of Richard Sellaway. 1764. W. B. 7, p. 363.

STEVENS, EDMUND and ELIZABETH PIERCE, daughter of John Pierce. 1784. D. B. 15, p. 375.

#STEVENS, JACOB and ANN COGGAN, daughter of Robert Coggan. 1737. W. B. 4, p. 218. D. B. 8, p. 189.

STEVENS, JACOB and MARTHA TOMLIN, daughter of Mathew Tomlin. 1763. D. B. 11, p. 161 & 192.

#STEVENS, JOHN and ELIZABETH COGGAN, daughter of Robert Coggan. 1737. W. B. 4, p. 218. W. B. 9, p. 244.

STEVENS, THOMAS of Brunswick County and LUCY BENNETT, daughter of John Bennett. 1774. O. B. 1772-80, p. 273. W. B. 8, p. 492.

STOIKES, ROBERT and JANE BRASWELL, daughter of Robert Braswell. 1667. W. & D. B. 2, p. 52 & 55.

STORY, THOMAS and ELIZABETH BRAGG, daughter of James Bragg. 1728. W. B. 3, p. 82.

STREET, MADDISON and MARGARET SURBY, daughter of John Surby. 1715. G. B., p. 90.

STRINGFIELD, BENJAMIN and MOURNING WOMBWELL, daughter of Thomas Wombwell. 1784. W. B. 9, p. 294.

STRINGFIELD, JAMES and ANN WOMBWELL, daughter of Thomas Wombwell. 1784. W. B. 9, p. 294.

#STROUD, JOHN and SARAH MORRIS, daughter of John Morris. 1759. W. B. 8, p. 197. O. B. 1759-63, p. 83.

STUART, JOHN and BETSEY SMITH. Marriage Contract. 1773. D. B. 13, p. 65.

SUMMERELL, GEORGE and JANE STEPHENSON, daughter of Thomas Stephenson. 1770. Southampton County W. B. 2, p. 314.

SUMMERELL, THOMAS and ELIZABETH STEPHENSON, daughter of Thomas Stephenson. 1770. Southampton County W. B. 2, p. 314.

SUMNER, HOLLAND of North Carolina and MARTHA NORSEWORTHY, daughter of Charles Norseworthy. 1773. D. B. 13, p. 117.

TABOUR, THOMAS and JUDITH ALLEN, daughter of Joseph Allen.
1751. W. B. 5, p. 392.

TALLOUGH, JAMES and MRS. ANN GRIFFIN, relict of Thomas Griffin.
1694. D. B. 1, p. 133.

TAYLOR, CHARLES B. and MRS. LUCY JONES, relict of Willis Jones.
1794. W. B. 11, p. 133.

TAYLOR, ETHELDRED and PATIENCE KINCHIN, daughter of William
Kinchin. 1734. W. B. 4, p. 72.

TAYLOR, JOHN and EASTER PITT, daughter of Henry Pitt. 1766.
D. B. 12, p. 120.

TAYLOR, KINCHIN and RIDLEY BROWNE, daughter of Jesse Browne.
1770. Southampton County W. B. 2, p. 357.

TAYLOR, THOMAS and ------- HARRIS, daughter of William Harris.
1747. D. B. 8, p. 135.

THOMAS, JACOB and MARY NORSEWORTHY, sister of Tristram Norseworthy. 1773. W. B. 8, p. 332.

THOMAS, JOHN and MRS. SUSANNA FRIZZELL, relict of John Frizzell.
1693. D. B. 1, p. 65.

THOMAS, JOHN and MARY LAWRENCE, daughter of John Lawrence.
1736. D. B. 5, p. 186.

THOMAS, JOHN and MARY MOODY, daughter of Phillip Moody. 1756.
D. B. 9, p. 474.

THOMAS, RICHARD and ELEANOR SHERRER, daughter of John Sherrer
(Sherwood). 1736. W. B. 4, p. 192. D. B. 9, p. 379.

#THOMAS, WILLIAM and ------- HILL, daughter of Mrs. Silvestra
Hill. 1695. W. & D. B. 2, p. 408. D. B. 1, p. 201.

THROPE, THOMAS and MRS. MARTHA LEWER, relict of William Lewer.
1685. W. & D. B. 2, (Rev.) p. 58.

THROPP, THOMAS and MRS. MARY FORD, relict of Joseph Ford.
1709. W. & D. B. 2, p.497.

THROPP, THOMAS and MARY LEWIS, daughter of Daniel Lewis. 1709.
W. & D. B. 2, p. 514 & 531.

TIBBOTT, RICHARD and MARY BRIDGER, daughter of Joseph Bridger.
1686. W. & D. B. 2, p. 254.

TODD, MALLORY and ANGELINA MALLORY, daughter of John Mallory.
1788. W. B. 10, p. 128 & 129.

TOLER, JOHN and MRS. JULIA PITT, relict of Henry Pitt. 1783.
O. B. 1780-83, p. 216.

TOMLIN, JOHN and CHARLOTTE HOLLAND, daughter of James Holland.
1801. O. B. 1801-3, p. 125.

TOMLIN, MATHEW and ------- WATSON, daughter of John Watson.

1685. W. & D. B. 2, p. 243.

TOMLIN, NICHOLAS and REBECCA JOHNSON, daughter of Robert Johnson. 1784. W. B. 9, p. 282. W. B. 11, p. 40.

TOULE, HERCULES and MRS. SUSANNAH REYNOLDS, relict of Richard Reynolds. 1708. D. B. 2, p. 102. W. & D. B. 2, p. 244.

TUEL, BIGNALL and MRS. SARAH GRAY, relict of Aaron Gray. 1758. W. B. 6, p. 197.

TUKE, JOHN and ELIZABETH SKELTON, daughter of Thomas Skelton. 1730. W. B. 3, p. 249.

TURNER, HENRY and ELIZABETH WILKINSON, daughter of Richard Wilkinson. 1715. W. & D. B. 2, p. 625.

TURNER, JACOB and PRISCILLA BLUNT, daughter of Benjamin Blunt. 1778. Southampton County W. B. 3, p. 435.

TURNER, JOHN and ------- TOMLIN, daughter of Mathew Tomlin. 1684. W. & D. B. 2, p. 264.

TURNER, JOHN and SARAH STREET, daughter of John Street. 1710. W. & D. B. 2, p. 523.

TURNER, THOMAS and MARTHA JOYNER, daughter of Thomas Joyner. 1719. G. B., p. 313.

TURNER, THOMAS and LUCRETIA SEAGRAVE, daughter of Francis Seagrave. 1725. W. B. 3, p. 56.

TURNER, WILLIAM and MARTHA EDWARDS, daughter of Solomon Edwards. 1777. D. B. 13, p. 490. W. B. 11, p. 205.

TYNES, HENRY and SARAH, granddaughter of Mrs. Sarah Crocker. 1781. W. B. 9, p. 66. W. B. 10, p. 99.

TYRRELL, BLACKEBY and SARAH JONES. Marriage Contract. 1698. D. B. 1, p. 267.

UZZELL, THOMAS and MARY PARR, daughter of Anthony Parr. 1779. O. B. 1772-80, p. 490 & 502.

UZZELL, THOMAS and NANCY MORRISON, daughter of William Morrison. 1804. O. B. 1803-6, p. 261. W. B. 11, p. 722.

VALENTINE, JAMES and MARY MIDLAND, daughter of George Midland. 1667. W. & D. B. 1, p. 118.

VANCE, HUGH and MRS. LYDIA PORTLOCK, relict of Charles Portlock. 1756. W. B. 6, p. 227. W. B. 5, p. 322 & 439.

#VANISER, PETER and ANN ALMAND, daughter of Isaac Almand. 1786. W. B. 10, p. 246.

VAUGHAN, HENRY and MRS. ANN BLOW, relict of Richard Blow Jr. 1746. O. B. 1747-52, p. 20. W. B. 5, p. 37.

VAUGHAN, THOMAS and MRS. MARGARET BOYKIN, relict of William
Boykin. 1734. W. B. 4, p. 44. W. B. 5, p. 89.

VELLINES, NATHANIEL and SALLY THOMAS, daughter of Phillip Thomas.
1812. O. B. 1810-13, p. 269.

VELLINES, TWAITE and MARY CLAYTON, daughter of John Clayton.
1756. W. B. 6, p. 458.

VIVIAN, THOMAS and ELIZABETH WILLIAMSON. 1672. W. & D. B. 2,
p. 107.

#WADE, SAMUEL and SUSANNA BARDEN, sister of John Barden. 1695.
D. B. 1, p. 190.

WAIKLEY, MATHEW and MRS. JULIAN STANTLIN, relict of Darby
Stantlin. 1670. W. & D. B. 2, p. 90.

#WAINWRIGHT, WILLIAM and MARY SUMMERELL, daughter of Thomas
Summerell. 1739. W. B. 4, p. 172 & 254.

WAKEFIELD, JOHN and MARY OLIVER, daughter of John Oliver.
1666. W. & D. B. 1, p. 94.

WAKEFIELD, THOMAS of Nansemond County and ELIZABETH DARDEN,
daughter of Mrs. Mourning Darden. 1779. D. B. 14,
p. 130.

WALKER, GEORGE and MRS. MARGARET WARREN, relict of David Warren.
1666. W. & D. B. 2, (Rev.) p. 12.

WALTERS, WALTER and MRS. ALICE LARIMORE, relict of Roger Larimore. 1687. W. & D. B. 2, (Rev.) p. 64 & 284.

WALTON, JOHN and MRS. ELIZABETH WYNNE, relict of Hugh Wynne.
1666. W. & D. B. 1, p. 87.

#WARD, JOHN WIATT of Nansemond County and SUSANNA MOORE, daughter
of Isaac Moore. 1785. D. B. 15, p. 649.

WARD, THOMAS and JOANNA RAYNER, daughter of Francis Rayner.
1719. G. B. 2, p. 9.

WARD, WILLIAM and MRS. SARAH LIGHTFOOT, relict of Bartholomew
Lightfoot Jr. 1780. W. B. 9, p. 53.

WARDROPER, JOHN of London and MRS. HESTER BROWN, relict of
James Brown. 1730. D. B. 4, p. 182.

WARREN, JOHN and SARAH DEBERRY, daughter of Peter Deberry.
1712. W. & D. B. 2, p. 554.

WARREN, ROBERT and MARGARET DAWSON, daughter of Martin Dawson.
1745. W. B. 5, p. 52.

WATERS, DANIEL and MRS. ------- BETHESEA, relict of Robert
Bethesea. 1672. W. & D. B. 2, (Rev.) p. 33.

WATKINS, WILLIAM and HONOUR BEAL, daughter of Absalom Beal.
1804. O. B. 1803-6, p. 148.

WATSON, JOHN and MRS. SARAH WEST, relict of Nicholas West.

1668. W. & D. B. 2, p. 58 & 108.

WATSON, JAMES and ------- WILSON, daughter of Samuel Wilson.
1789. W. B. 10, p. 137.

WATTS, JOHN and ALICE ENGLISH, daughter of John English.
1678. W. & D. B. 2, p. 166.

WAUGH, JOHN and ELIZABETH MADISON, daughter of Richard Madison.
1676. W. & D. B. 2, p. 155.

WEBB, JAMES and ELIZABETH GODWIN, daughter of Thomas Godwin.
1675. W. & D. B. 2, (Rev.) p. 39.

WEBB, MATHEW and ANN BARLOW, daughter of William Barlow.
1780. W. B. 9, p. 64 & 302. W. B. 11, p. 185.

WEBB, SAMUEL and SUSANNA HARRISON, daughter of John Harrison.
1746. D. B. 7, p. 453.

WEBB, SAMUEL of Surry County and ANN APPLEWHAITE, daughter of
Arthur Applewhaite. 1772. D. B. 12, p. 499. D. B.
15, p. 422.

WEBB, WILLIAM and MARY TABERER, daughter of Thomas Taberer.
1692. W. & D. B. 2, p. 350.

WELCH, JOHN and MRS. MARY DELK, relict of John Delk. 1760.
O. B. 1759-63, p. 147. W. B. 6, p. 72.

WELCH, WILLIAM and SARAH BATTEN, daughter of Daniel Batten.
1702. W. & D. B. 2, p. 459 & 464.

WENTWORTH, SAMUEL and MARY CALCOTE, daughter of Thomas Calcote
(Calclough). 1739. D. B. 5, p. 349.

WEST, HENRY and ------- FULGHAM, daughter of Michael Fulgham.
1727. W. B. 3, p. 59.

WEST, JACOBY and MRS. SILVIA BRANTLEY, relict of John Brantley.
1762. O. B. 1759-63, p. 354.

WEST, NICHOLAS and MRS. SARAH LUKE, relict of Paul Luke.
1667. W. & D. B. 2, p. 59.

WEST, RICHARD and ELIZABETH PITT, sister of John Pitt. 1781.
W. B. 9, p. 71.

WEST, WILLIAM and REBECCA BRASWELL, daughter of Robert Braswell.
1668. W. & D. B. 2, p. 52 & 55.

WESTON, BENJAMIN and MRS. ISABELLA FULGHAM, relict of Nicholas
Fulgham. 1738. W. B. 4, p. 142 & 253. D. B. 7, p. 288.

WESTON, JOHN and ANN SMITH, daughter of William Smith. 1690.
W. & D. B. 2, p. 300 & 470.

WESTON, JOHN of Nansemond County and ISABELLA PARKER, daughter
of George Parker. 1750. D. B. 8, p. 340.

WESTRAY, ARTHUR and ELIZABETH GODWIN, daughter of John Godwin.
1762. D. B. 11, p. 20.

WESTRAY, BENJAMIN and ELIZABETH SAWYER. 1763. D. B. 11,
p. 192.

WESTRAY, JOHN and ANN EXUM, daughter of Robert Exum. 1751.
D. B. 8, p. 422.

WHEADON, JOSEPH and MRS. JOYCE CARRELL, relict of Samuel Carrell.
1745. W. B. 4, p. 288 & 528.

WHEADON, PHILLIP and MRS. SARAH LUCKS, relict of John Lucks.
1724. G. B., p. 646.

WHITAKER, PHINEAS and ------- MOORE, daughter of John Moore.
1722. G. B., p. 510. W. & D. B. 2, p. 279.

WHITE, ANTHONY and MARY PITT, daughter of Henry Pitt. 1766.
D. B. 12, p. 120.

WHITE, JOHN of Lower Norfolk County and EADY LLEWELLEN, daughter
of Thomas Llewellen. 1664. W. & D. B. 1, p. 22.

WHITE, SAMUEL of Norfolk and BETHIAH BIRD, daughter of Mrs.
Elizabeth Bird. 1773. D. B. 13, p. 88.

WHITE, THOMAS and ANN MOORE, daughter of George Moore. 1710.
W. & D. B. 2, p. 586. W. B. 4, p. 401 & 409.

WHITE, THOMAS and ------- HARRISON, daughter of John Harrison.
1722. W. B. 3, p. 318.

#WHITEHEAD, ARTHUR and MARY GODWIN, daughter of William Godwin.
1710. G. B. 2, p. 52. W. & D. B. 2, p. 528.

WHITEHEAD, ARTHUR and ISABELLA PURSELL, daughter of Arthur
Pursell. 1717. W. B. 3, p. 163.

WHITEHEAD, JOSEPH of North Carolina and PHERIBA APPLEWHAITE,
daughter of John Applewhaite. 1771. D. B. 12, p. 487.

WHITFIELD, MATHEW of Nansemond County and PRISCILLA LAWRENCE,
daughter of John Lawrence. 1708. D. B. 2, p.115.

WHITFIELD, MATHEW and MRS. RACHEL NORSEWORTHY, relict of John
Norseworthy. 1746. O. B. 1746-52, p. 10.

WHITFIELD, SAMUEL and NANCY HUNT, daughter of Joshua Hunt.
1805. O. B. 1803-5, p. 378.

WHITFIELD, THOMAS and MARY HARRISON, daughter of William Harrison. 1751. D. B. 8, p. 401.

WHITFIELD, THOMAS and MRS. MARY DICKENSON, relict of Jacob
Dickenson. 1755. W. B. 14, (Rev.) p. 16.

WHITFIELD, WILLIAM and MARY COPELAND, sister of Thomas Copeland.
1741. W. B. 4, p. 402. D. B. 14, (Rev.) p. 55.

WHITLEY, JOHN and ------- MADDEN, sister of Henry Madden.
1687. W. & D. B. 2, (Rev.) p. 61.

WHITLEY, JOSEPH and MARY SHAW, daughter of Mrs. Elizabeth Shaw.
1752. W. B. 6, p. 28.

WHITLEY, THOMAS and MARY STREET, daughter of John Street. 1710.
W. & D. B. 2, p. 523 & 615.

WHITLEY, THOMAS and SUSANNAH FULGHAM, daughter of Nicholas
Fulgham. 1719. G. B. 2, p. 170.

WIGGS, HENRY and CATHERINE LUKE, daughter of Paul Luke. 1754.
D. B. 9, p. 240.

WILDS, THOMAS and ANN KING, sister of Robert King. 1675.
W. & D. B. 2, p. 434. (Rev.) p. 35.

WILKINSON, COFIELD and MRS. JENNIE LOWRY, relict of Isaac Lowry.
1802. O. B. 1801-3, p. 221.

WILKINSON, WILLIAM and ELIZABETH WEBB, daughter of James Webb.
1717. W. & D. B. 2, p. 619.

WILKINSON, WILLIAM and REBECCA POWELL, daughter of William
Powell. 1734. W. B. 4, p. 46. D. B. 9, p. 343.

#WILLIAMS, ARTHUR of North Carolina and HANNAH MANDEW, daughter
of Thomas Mandew. 1737. D. B. 5, p. 152.

WILLIAMS, DAVID and ANN GRAY, sister of Mourning Gray. 1740.
W. B. 8, p. 349. D. B. 5, p. 498.

WILLIAMS, DENNIS and MRS. ------- ALTMAN, relict of John Altman.
1694. D. B. 1, (Rev.) p. 51.

WILLIAMS, EPAPHRODITUS and RACHEL WILKINSON, sister of Richard
Wilkinson. 1728. W. B. 3, p. 123.

WILLIAMS, GEORGE and NANCY HOUGH, sister of John Hough. 1802.
O. B. 1801-3, p. 152.

WILLIAMS, JACOB and MARTHA DRAKE, daughter of Richard Drake.
1759. Southampton County W. B. 1, p. 313.

WILLIAMS, JOHN and ------- WHITLEY, daughter of John Whitley.
1671. W. & D. B. 2, p. 105.

WILLIAMS, JOHN and MARY PARNELL, sister of Thomas Parnell.
1687. W. & D. B. 2, p. 278.

WILLIAMS, JOHN and MRS. SARAH COOPER, relict of Robert Cooper.
1694. D. B. 1, (Rev.) p. 47.

WILLIAMS, JOHN and ------- WAINWRIGHT, sister of William Wainwright. 1769. W. B. 8, p. 204.

WILLIAMS, PETER and MARY GREEN, daughter of John Green. 1719.
G. B., p. 261.

WILLIAMS, RICHARD and OLIVE DRIVER, daughter of Giles Driver.
1777. D. B. 13, p. 518.

WILLIAMS, THOMAS and MRS. SUSANNAH DAVIS, relict of John Davis.
1726. W. B. 3, p. 37.

WILLIAMS, THOMAS of North Carolina and MRS. SARAH WARREN, relict
of Thomas Warren. 1750. Southampton County D. B. 1,
p. 81.

#WILLIAMS, WILLIAM and REBECCA ELEY, daughter of Robert Eley.
1738. W. B. 4, p. 233. W. B. 6, p. 135.

WILLIAMS, WILLIAM and MARY DRAKE, daughter of Thomas Drake.
1757. Southampton County W. B. 1, p. 254.

WILLIAMSON, ARTHUR and ANN EXUM, sister of Francis Exum.

1752. W. B. 5, p. 451. Southampton County W. B. 1,
p. 127.

WILLIAMSON, FRANCIS of North Carolina and SUSANNAH CLAYTON,
daughter of John Clayton. 1756. W. B. 6, p. 458.
D. B. 8, p. 314.

WILLIAMSON, GEORGE and HESTER BRIDGER, daughter of Joseph
Bridger. 1721. D. B. 9, p. 172.

WILLIAMSON, GEORGE and FRANCES DAVIS, daughter of Thomas Davis.
1721. G. B. 2, p. 114.

WILLIAMSON, JAMES and ANN UNDERWOOD, sister of William Underwood. 1652. Bk. A, p. 38.

WILLIAMSON, ROBERT and JOAN ALLEN, daughter of Arthur Allen
of Surry County. 1669. W. & D. B. 2, p. 85.

WILLIAMSON, THOMAS and OLIVE EXUM, sister of Francis Exum.
1752. W. B. 5, p. 451. Southampton County W. B. 1,
p. 127.

WILLS, JOHN and MARTHA CASEY, daughter of Richard Casey.
1745. W. B. 5, p. 112.

WILLS, MILES and MARY APPLEWHAITE, sister of Ann Applewhaite.
1757. W. B. 6, p. 312.

WILLS, PARKER and ESTHER PEDIN, sister of Edmund Pedin.
1811. O. B. 1810-13, p. 133.

WILLS, THOMAS and ANN MORELAND, sister of John Moreland.
1770. D. B. 12, p. 390.

WILLS, WILLIS and CONSTANCE HARRISON, sister of Elizabeth Harrison. 1798. W. B. 11, p. 140.

WILSON, GOODRICH and LOIS WENTWORTH, daughter of Samuel Wentworth. 1767. D. B. 15, p. 140.

WILSON, JAMES and MRS. MARY DICKINSON, relict of Jacob Dickinson.
1761. D. B. 12, p. 260.

WILSON, JOSIAH of Surry County and MRS. MARTHA WRENN, relict of
Francis Wrenn. 1782. W. B. 10, p. 176. D. B. 15,
p. 246.

WILSON, NICHOLAS and MARGARET SAMPSON, daughter of James Sampson.
1688. W. & D. B. 2, p. 291.

WILSON, SAMUEL and MRS. MARGARET MILLER, relict of William Miller. 1752. W. B. 6, p. 13. O. B. 1759-63, p. 484.

WILSON, WILLIS and SARAH BLUNT, daughter of William Blunt.
1780. W. B. 9, p. 45. O. B. 1780-3, p. 1.

WINBORNE, JOHN of Nansemond County and PHOEBE, granddaughter of
Phoebe Kirle. 1751. D. B. 8, p. 392.

WOODLEY, TOMAS and MRS. FRANCES WILSON, relict of John Wilson.
1720. W. B. 3, p. 121.

WOODSIDE, JOHN of Norfolk and JANE BIRD, daughter of Mrs. Elizabeth Bird. 1773. D. B. 13, p. 88.

WOODWARD, JOHN GEORGE and ESTHER KING, sister of John King.
1797. W. B. 11, p. 146.

WOODWARD, WILLIAM and JEAN SMELLEY, daughter of John Smelley.
1765. W. B. 7, p. 369. W. B. 8, p. 361.

WOODWARD, WILLIAM and ANN HALL, daughter of George Hall.
1779. D. B. 14, p. 116.

WOMBWELL, JOSEPH and MRS. JOANNA CLARK, relict of Joseph Clark.
1763. O. B. 1759-63, p. 473.

WOMBWELL, LEMUEL and MRS. ALICE CALCOTE, relict of Harwood
Calcote. 1802. O. B. 1801-3, p. 368.

WOORY, JOSEPH and MRS. ELIZABETH WEBB, relict of James Webb.
1693. W. & D. B. 2, p. 336.

WOOTTEN, RICHARD and LUCY COUNCIL, sister of Hodges Council.
1730. D. B. 4, p. 98.

WORRELL, RICHARD and DORCAS REYNOLDS, daughter of Henry Reynolds.
1715. W. & D. B. 2, p. 609.

WORRELL, RICHARD and HONOUR MARKS, daughter of Thomas Marks.
1771. Southampton County W. B. 2, p. 466.

WRENN, FRANCIS and MRS. MARTHA HARRISON, relict of Henry Harrison. 1775. O. B. 1772-80, p. 319.

WRENN, JOSIAH and ------- MALLICOTE, daughter of George Mallicote. 1798. W. B. 11, p. 455.

WRENN, JOHN and PRUDENCE DAVIS, sister of Thomas Davis. 1734.
W. B. 4, p. 23. W. B. 5, p. 233.

WRENN, THOMAS and CATHERINE INGRAM, daughter of Jennings Ingram.
1771. D. B. 12, p. 428.

WRIGHT, JOHN and JULIANA WILLIAMS, sister of Epaphroditus Williams. 1728. W. B. 3, p. 123. W. B. 4, p. 422.

#WRIGHT, JOSEPH and MRS. MARY BENN, relict of Capt. James Benn.
1741. W. B. 3, p. 340. W. B. 4, p. 405.

WRIGHT, THOMAS and ELIZABETH WILLIAMS, daughter of John Williams.
1691. W. & D. B. 2, p. 317 & 433. D. B. 1, p. 105.

WRIGHT, WILLIAM and ANN BLUNT, daughter of William Blunt.
1787. Southampton County W. B. 4, p. 232.

WYNNE, HUGH and MRS. ------- COBB, relict of George Cobb.
1666. W. & D. B. 1, p. 87.

ADDITIONAL LIST OF MARRIAGES

ALLEN, EDWARD and MRS. ELIZABETH DRIVER, relict of John Driver. 1795. O. B. 1795-97, p. 214.

ASKEW, WILLIAM and ELIZABETH WILKINSON, daughter of Henry Wilkinson. 1721. G. B., p. 430.

BENNETT, JOHN and SARAH WELCH, sister of John Welch. 1769. W. B. 8, p. 61 & 127.

BLUNT, WILLIAM and MOLLY WOODLEY, daughter of John Woodley. 1791. W. B. 10, p. 214.

BOON, JAMES and SARAH RAIFORD, daughter of William Raiford. 1766. W. B. 8, p. 269. D. B. 12, p. 91.

BOON, RATCLIFF and MARY RAIFORD, daughter of William Raiford. 1771. W. B. 8, p. 269 & 492.

BOWCOCK, PETER and JANE ABIGAIL ABBINGTON. 1774. D. B. 13, p. 256. W. B. 8, p. 526.

BOWEN, JOHN JR. and MARY WARREN, daughter of Thomas Warren. 1750. Southampton County D. B. 1, p. 81.

BRADDY, WILLIAM and CATHERINE FLAKE, daughter of Robert Flake. 1718. G. B., p. 191. D. B. 6, p. 240.

BRITT, BRITAIN and MRS. JANE EDMUNDS, relict of James Edmunds. 1797. (See Marriage Bonds) O. B. 1795-97, p. 297. O. B. 1797-1801, p. 146.

#BROWN, JAMES and PATIENCE RODWAY, daughter of John Rodway. 1750. W. B. 5, p. 427. D. B. 14, (Rev.) p. 169.

BROWN, THOMAS and ELIZABETH TYNES, sister of West Tynes. 1779. O. B. 1772-80, p. 473.

BROWN, WILLIAM and DOLLY JORDAN, daughter of Josiah Jordan. 1786. W. B. 10, p. 30.

CARR, DEMPSEY and ------- ENGLISH, daughter of Mrs. Mary English. 1774. W. B. 8, p. 475.

#CARR, JOSHUA and MARY APPLEWHAITE, daughter of Arthur Applewhaite. 1779. W. B. 9, p. 62. D. B. 15, p. 423.

CARSTAPHEN, JOHN and MRS. MARTHA SAUNDERS, relict of Henry Saunders. 1773. W. B. 8, p. 278.

CHAPPELL, JAMES and ELIZABETH BRIGGS, daughter of Henry Briggs. 1721. D. B. 6, p. 353. G. B., p. 420.

CLAYTON, WILLIAM and PRISCILLA BRIGGS, daughter of James Briggs. 1756. W. B. 6, p. 268. W. B. 8, p. 504.

COFER, THOMAS JR. and ELIZABETH WOMBLE, daughter of Joseph Womble. 1775. W. B. 9, p. 206. D. B. 13, p. 395.

CROOM, EDWARD and SARAH RICHARDS, daughter of Robert Richards. 1733. W. B. 3, p. 377. (See William and Mary Quarterly 2nd S. Vol. 10, p. 257.)

COLLINS, JOHN and MARY SKINNER, widow. 1680. W. & D. B. 1, p. 439 & 443.

CUTCHINS, JOSEPH and PRISCILLA PITT, daughter of John Pitt. 1775. W. B. 7, p. 61. D. B. 15, p. 221, 308, 315, & 328.

DARDEN, POWER and MRS. MOURNING BURK, relict of John Burk. 1760. O. B. 1759-63, p. 138.

DICK, DAVID and ANN WODDROP, sister of Alexander Woddrop. 1795. O. B. 1795-97, p. 7.

EDMUNDS, JAMES and MRS. JANE NORSWORTHY, relict of John Norsworthy. 1795. W. B. 10, p. 322. O. B. 1795-97, p. 297. O. B. 1797-1801, p. 27.

EDWARDS, HEZEKIAH and MARY SMITH, sister of Virgus Smith. 1774. W. B. 8, p. 328.

FULGHAM, ALLEN and NANCY FULGHAM, daughter of Edmund Fulgham. 1798. O. B. 1797-1801, p. 320.

GARRETT, LAZARUS and ELIZABETH SHIVERS, daughter of Robert Shivers. 1750. Southampton County D. B. 1, p. 87.

GRAY, HENRY and CONNY WOMBLE, daughter of Britain Womble. 1797. O. B. 1795-97, p. 523.

GWALTNEY, THOMAS of North Carolina and MARTHA GOODMAN, daughter of William Goodman. 1737. D. B. 5, p. 111. D. B. 10, p. 68.

HANCOCK, JAMES and CHACEY WOMBLE, daughter of Britain Womble. 1797. O. B. 1795-97, p. 523.

HARRIS, MICHAEL and SARAH COOK, sister of John Cook. 1762. W. B. 8, p. 457.

HARRISON, SAMPSON and COMFORT JONES, sister of Willis Jones. 1795. O. B. 1795-97, p. 37.

HOUGH, JAMES of Gloucester County and MARTHA HOLLEMAN. 1763. Southampton County W. B. 2, p. 136. D. B. 14, p. 1.

HOWARD, WILLIAM and ELIZABETH EMSON, daughter of Thomas Emson. 1678. W. & D. B. 2, p. 169.

HUNTER, JOSHUA and MARY COVINGTON GROSS, daughter of Thomas Gross. 1742. W. B. 4, p. 426. D. B. 9, p. 259.

JORDAN, JOHN and ELIZABETH WAINWRIGHT, sister of William Wainwright. 1769. W. B. 8, p. 204. W. B. 10, p. 187.

JORDAN, WILLIAM and MRS. MARTHA MARSHALL, relict of Robert
     Marshall. 1797. O. B. 1797-1801, p. 23. (See
     Marriage Bonds.)

JOYNER, BRIDGEMAN and DEBORAH HARDY, daughter of John Hardy.
     1713. D. B. 2, p. 306. W. & D. B. 2, p. 146, 166 & 590.

KING, HENRY and MARTHA NORSWORTHY, sister of Tristram Norsworthy.
     1767. W. B. 8, p. 186.

LAIN, BENJAMIN and ANN DREW, daughter of Edward Drew. 1745.
     Southampton County W. B. 1, p. 8.

LEVY, LAZARUS and MRS. KEZIAH MALLORY HARVEY, daughter of John
     Mallory. 1796. (See Marriage Bonds.) W. B. 10,
     p. 128. O. B. 1795-97, p. 471.

LEVY, LAZARUS and MRS. SARAH (HODSDEN) DRUMMOND, relict of
     William Hodsden. 1795. (See Marriage Bonds.)
     O. B. 1797-1801, p. 21 & 278.

LITTLE, JAMES and HARTY WOMBLE, daughter of Britain Womble.
     1797. O. B. 1795-97, p. 523.

LOYD, THOMAS and PATIENCE EXUM, daughter of Thomas Exum.
     1748. D. B. 8, p. 186.

MARSHALL, ROBERT and MARTHA WATSON, daughter of James Watson.
     1796. O. B. 1795-97, p. 481. O. B. 1797-1801, p. 23.

MARSTON, JOHN and MRS. SUSANNAH DUNLOP, relict of Archibald
     Dunlop. 1795. O. B. 1795-97, p. 73.

#MERCER, ROBERT and MRS. ELIZABETH DUKE, relict of John Duke.
     1689. D. B. 1, p. 25 & 88.

#MURRELL, GEORGE of North Carolina and MARY MAYO, daughter of
     William Mayo. 1754. D. B. 9, p. 209. D. B. 6, p. 206.

NEWBY, THOMAS and MARY LAWRENCE, daughter of John Lawrence.
     1772. W. B. 8, p. 151. O. B. 1772-80, p. 339.

NORSWORTHY, TRISTRAM and MRS. ANNE GODWIN, relict of Edmond
     Godwin. 1798. O. B. 1797-1801, p. 396.

PHILLIPS, MARK and ELIZABETH BOWLES. 1796. O. B. 1795-97,
     p. 360.

PLEASANTS, WILLIAM and MARTHA BARLOW, sister of Sampson Barlow.
     1798. O. B. 1797-1801, p. 347.

POPE, HARDY and SALLY WESTRAY, daughter of Robert Westray.
     1798. O. B. 1797-1801, p. 389.

POPE, JOHN and ELIZABETH POWELL, daughter of William Powell.
     1749. D. B. 8, p. 265.

PROVANS, HUGH and ANN SMELLY, daughter of John Smelly. 1775.
     W. B. 8, p. 361. W. B. 7, p. 369.

REVELL, JOHN and SARAH FAIRCLOTH, daughter of William Faircloth.
     1731. D. B. 4, p. 129.

#ROGERD, JOHN of North Carolina and BRIDGETT COOK, sister of
     Isaac Cook. 1722. G. B., p. 500. W. B. 3, p. 63.

SAUNDERS, ELIAS and MARTHA WATKINS, daughter of Jesse Watkins. 1795. O. B. 1795-97, p. 19.

SHELLY, JOHN and PATSEY WEBB, daughter of Mathais Webb. 1797. O. B. 1795-97, p. 522. W. B. 9, p. 302.

SMITH, THOMAS and ELIZABETH WODDROP, sister of Alexander Woddrop. 1795. O. B. 1795-97, p. 7.

SOUTHALL, JAMES B. and MARY WHITFIELD, daughter of Thomas Whitfield. 1799. O. B. 1797-1801, p. 557 & 563.

STEPHENSON, EDMUND and SALLY BRITT, daughter of Benjamin Britt. 1783. Southampton County W. B. 4, p. 95.

STEPHENSON, JOHN and CATHERINE WIGGS, daughter of Henry Wiggs. 1729. W. B. 3, p. 184. W. B. 4, p. 162.

WATSON, MICHAEL and BATHSHEBA HOLLAND, sister of Elijah Holland. 1795. O. B. 1795-97, p. 20.

WILLIAMS, JOHN and MRS. ELIZABETH TABERER COPELAND, daughter of Thomas Taberer. 1696. D. B. 1, p. 223. W. & D. B. 2, p. 350.

WILLIAMS, JOHN and ROSE MICHAELS, daughter of John Michaels. 1795. O. B. 1795-97, p. 21. W. B. 10, p. 276.

WILLS, MOSES and PATIENCE CHAPMAN, daughter of John Chapman. 1736. W. B. 4, p. 183. (See William and Mary Quarterly, 2nd S., Vol. 10, p. 256.)

WHITFIELD, WILSON and MRS. FRANCES MILLER, relict of Robert Miller. 1780. O. B. 1795-97, p. 359. W. B. 9, p. 57.

WOODSON, JOSEPH of Henrico County and ELIZABETH MURRY, daughter of John Murry. 1724. G. B. 2, p. 166. D. B. 4, p. 354.

WOMBLE, BRITAIN and HARTY CASEY, daughter of Nicholas Casey. 1763. W. B. 7, p. 244. O. B. 1795-97, p. 523.

#WOMBWELL, THOMAS and ELIZABETH WOOD, daughter of John Wood and daughter-in-law of Thomas Taberer. 1696. W. & D. B. 2, p. 275 & 350. Minute Book - Lower Virginia Meeting, p. 73.

MARRIAGE BONDS

ADDISON, WILLIAM and NANCY GRAY   August 11, 1800

ALLMOND, JAMES and MARY MORRISON   February 1, 1791
    Surety, James Young

ALLMOND, WILLIAM and ELIZABETH TOLLER   December 26, 1795
    Surety, James Garner

APPLEWHAITE, JOHN and MARTHA WILLS   August 7, 1783
    Surety, Mills Wills

APPLEWHAITE, JOSIAH and POLLY GIBBS (alias WHITFIELD)
    Surety, Joseph Driver   December 4, 1787

ARMSTRONG, JOHN and UNITY BRANTLEY   October 21, 1787
    Surety, Lemuel Godfrey

ASKEW, AARON and ELIZABETH NEWMAN   August 6, 1792
    Surety, Joseph Matthews

ASKEW, JONAS and POLLY GARNER   July 14, 1791
    Surety, Joseph Matthews
    Witness, Benjamin Beal

ASKEW, MILLS and NANCY NEWMAN   February 17, 1800
    Guardian, William Godfrey

ATKINSON, JAMES and MARTHA APPLEWHAITE   March 27, 1790
    Guardian, Arthur Applewhaite

ATKINSON, JAMES and MILLY MALLICOTE (widow)   January 24, 1792
    Surety, William Atkinson

ATKINSON, JESSE and MARY WARD   August 25, 1791
    Surety, Francis Young

ATKINSON, JOHN and ELIZABETH GALE   April 27, 1798
    Surety, John Parker

BABB, WILLIAM and SILVIA BALDWIN   June 5, 1783
    Surety, William Baldwin
    Witness, Francis Young

BABB, WILLIAM and NANCY HARRELL   February 3, 1796
    Surety, Richard Outland

BAGNALL, WILLIAM and MATILDA DOWTY   August 29, 1791
    Surety, Addison Dowty

BAILEY, LEMUEL and BETSEY ELLIOTT   May 11, 1791
    Surety, Willis Jones
    Witness, Francis Young Jr.

BAINS, GEORGE and MARTHA W. REYNOLDS   November --, 1787
    Surety, Charles Groce
    Guardian, James Wills

BAINS, HENRY and FANNY CHANNELL   June 4, 1793
    Surety, Joshua Hunt
    Consent of Mildred Channell

BAKER, JOSEPH and JEMIMA STRINGFIELD   March 22, 1796
    Surety, Joseph Stringfield
    Parent, James Stringfield

BALDWIN, WILLIAM and ANN BABB   June 5, 1783
    Surety, William Eley
    Witness, Francis Young

BALLARD, ANDREW and LYDIA ELEY   October 5, 1795
    Surety, William Eley
    Parent, Milly Eley

BANKS, BENJAMIN and NANCY JONES   July 13, 1793
    Surety, Francis Young Jr.
    Witness, Willis Jones

BANKS, NATHANIEL and ELIZABETH M. WILLIS   July 20, 1795
    Surety, Davis Jones

BARLOW, BENJAMIN and FRANCES JONES   January 21, 1792
    Surety, David Jones

BARLOW, JAMES and MARY GIBBS   February 7, 1792
    Father-in-law, William Patterson

BARLOW, JOHN and SALLY WRENN   September 7, 1795
    Parent, Josiah Wrenn
    Uncle of John Barlow, Thomas Barlow
    Witness, Mathew Cofer

BARLOW, SAMPSON and LUCY BARLOW   September 15, 1798
    Surety, James Barlow

BARRAUD, PHILLIP, Doctor of Physick,. from   July 23, 1783
    the City of Williamburg and
    ANN H-------.
    Surety, Thomas Pierce
    Witness, Thomas Pierce Jr. and
    Samuel Brown

BASS, THOMAS and SARAH ENGLISH   January 25, 1788
    Surety, Francis Vaughan
    Parent, William English

BATTEN, SAMUEL and ---- MERCER   November 6, 1797
    Surety, Allen Johnson
    Parent, James Mercer

BEAL, ELIAS and AMEY CARR   May 3, 1790
    Surety, Thomas Johnson
    Consent of Elizabeth Carr and
    Priscilla Beal

BEATMAN, JOHN and TABITHA WHITLEY   June 4, 1793
    Surety, Henry Howard

BELL, MICAJAH and FRANCES MANGAM   April 19, 1800
    Surety, Patrick Gwaltney

BENNETT, JAMES and ANN WRIGHT   June 22, 1795
    Surety, John Dobbs

BENNETT, WILLIAM and ANN EDWARDS   November 23, 1793
    Surety, Mathew Turner

BEST, THOMAS and POLLY SHIVERS   March 20, 1793
    Surety, William Shivers

BIDGOOD, BENJAMIN and MARY DAVIS   October 5, 1796
    Surety, Josiah Davis

BIDGOOD, JAMES and NANCY DEW   November 21, 1792
    Surety, John Peirce

BIDGOOD, SAMUEL and MARY CARRELL   April 6, 1787
    Surety, John Murry

BLAND, THOMAS and MARY WALLER (widow)   December 2, 1791
    Surety, Francis Young
    Parent, Britton Wombwell
    Witness, Edmund Mason

BOLDS, THOMAS and MRS. LEODOWICK SMITH   March 19, 1800

BONES, SAMPSON and DOLLY BOWZER   June 1, 1787
    Surety, Scott Hollowell
    Witness, Bennett Young

BOON, SION and NANCY W. KEMP   January 7, 1793
    Surety, William Eley

BORLAND (BALDING), JOHN and ELIZABETH McCOY May 5, 1783
    Surety, Samuel McCoy

BOWEN, GEORGE and ANNA FATHEREE   September 29, 1795
    Surety, Fairfax Fatheree

BOYCE, DANIEL and PEGGY MANGAM   March 29, 1783
    Surety, Francis Young
    Parent, Micajah Mangam
    Witness, Josiah Mangam, Emanuel
    Hunter and Francis Young Jr.

BOYD, THOMAS and MILLY HUTCHINGS   April 28, 1788
    Surety, John Deford
    Witness, Francis Young

BOYKIN, WILLIAM and WILMUTH JORDAN   March 14, 1798
    Surety, William Patrick

BRADLEY, ABRAHAM and ANN WILSON   February 23, 1791
    Surety, James Wilson

BRADLEY, DAVID and ELIZABETH HARRISON (widow) May 30, 1791
    Surety, Harwood Callcote

BRADSHAW, ELIAS and ISABEL McINTOSH   March 2, 1795
    Surety, Jonas Bradshaw

BRANTLEY, DAVIS and ELIZABETH HARRISON   May 1, 1791

BRANTLEY, THOMAS and MARY LUPO   December 24, 1792
        Surety, VAlentine Brantley

BRANTLEY, THOMAS and REBECCA OUTLAND (widow)   January 6, 1798
        Surety, James Barlow

BRASWELL, GEORGE and CONNY COFER   January 21, 1791
        Surety, Francis Young

BRIDGER, JAMES ALLEN and ISABEL WHITEHEAD   January 29, 1783
        Surety, Robert Watkins
        Witness, Francis Young and
        William Bridger

BRIDGER, JAMES and BETSEY HERRING   September 4, 1797
        Surety, Allen Fulgham
        Witness, Elias Herring

BRIDGER, JOHN and ----- POWELL   February 7, 1784
        Surety, John Godwin
        Witness, Francis Young

BRITT, BRITTON and JENNY EDMONDS   February 6, 1797
        Surety, Joseph Britt
        Britton Britt from Southampton County

BRITT, JAMES and ELIZABETH HARRIS   September 26, 1787
        Surety, Thomas Bounds

BROADFIELD, CHARLES and CATHERINE PENNY   January 15, 1783
        Surety, Thomas Wills
        Witness, Francis Wills

BROADFIELD, JOHN and SARAH SMITH   October 8, 1784
        Surety, Lemuel Lightfoot
        Consent of Jonathan Godwin

BROCK, WILLIAM and MARY BRISTER   June 10, 1800
        Surety, James Deford

BROWN, G. A. and ABBY TUCKER   March 7, 1795
        Surety, Edward Wright
        Parent, Caty Tucker

BROWN, JOHN JR. and EMILY WHITLEY   October 6, 1798
        Surety, John Giles

BROWN, JOSEPH and CATHERINE PARNALL   May 18, 1787
        Surety, Samuel Bradley

BRYANT, CHARLES and CHARLOTTE STUCKIE   June 15, 1795
        Guardian, William Bryant

BRYANT, WILLIAM and ELIZABETH STUCKIE (widow)   September 27, 1791
        Surety, Thomas Flint

BULLOCK, OBADIAH and MARY JOHNSON   July 31, 1795
        Surety, Thomas Johnson

BUTLER, JACOB and PATIENCE TURNER   March 7, 1796
        Surety, John Holland

BUTLER, SOLOMON and POLLY RAWLES   January 5, 1795
        Surety, Willis Lankford

BUTLER, STEPHEN and JULIET HOLLAND   October 27, 1795
    Surety, Eley Johnson

BUTLER, WILLIS and ELIZABETH JOHNSON   March 20, 1790
    Surety, Eley Johnson
    Parent, Stephen Butler
    Michael and Elizabeth Johnson

CAMPBELL, WILLIAM and NANCY WAIL   December 6, 1796
    Surety, William Coffield
    Consent of Nancy Wail

CARR, JACOB and ELIZABETH BRADSHAW   April 17, 1783
    Surety, John Darden Jr.
    Witness, Francis Young

CARR, ROBERT and ANN HOLLEMAN   August 17, 1795
    Surety, Benjamin Brock
    Parent, Elizabeth Holleman
    Witness, James Young

CARR, SOLOMON and NANCY DAVIS   July 24, 1798
    Surety, Thomas Davis
    Parent, Edward Davis

CARR, WILLIAM and REBECCA DANIEL   April 6, 1795
    Surety, Jonas Bradshaw

CARRELL, THOMAS and JULIA UZZELL   September 6, 1790
    Surety, John Pinhorn

CARRELL, WILLIAM and CHARITY WOMBWELL   December 6, 1795
    Surety, James Carrell
    Witness, Edwin Wombwell

CARSON, RICHARD and ELIZABETH HOLLAND   January 9, 1792
    Surety, Jobe Holland

CARSTAPHEN, PERKINS and ELIZABETH SAUNDERS   March 17, 1788
    Surety, Henry Saunders

CARTER, JOHN (Cabinet Maker) and MARY SMITH   May 24, 1773
    Surety, Josiah Parker
    Parent, Joseph Smith Jr.
    Witness, Arthur Smith and
    John Goodrich

CASEY, JAMES and BETSEY WHITLEY   March 1, 1792
    Surety, Nathan Whitley
    Witness, Edmund Mason

CASEY, THOMAS and CELIA WALLACE   December 23, 1791
    Surety, John Atkins

CAWSON, JOHN and MARTHA CASEY (widow)   January 14, 1783
    Surety, Wilson Whitfield
    Witness, Francis Young

CHAPMAN, HARDY and SALLY JOHNSON   February 3, 1793
    Surety, Richard Chapman
    Parent, James Johnson

CHAPMAN, LEWIS and LUCY MANGAM   January 30, 1790

Surety, Francis Young
Parent, Micajah Mangam
Witness, Samuel Mangam and
Josiah Mangam

CLARK, JOHN and PEGGY NORSEWORTHY   October 7, 1786

CLARK, JOHN and ANNE GODWIN   June 4, 1793
    Surety, Mills Wills

CLARK, JOHN and BETSEY HUDSON   June 5, 1797

CLARK, LEMUEL and MARY WILLIAMS   January 29, 1795
    Surety, David Jones

CLARK, WILLIAM and SALLY GWALTNEY   December 14, 1790
    Surety, Patrick Gwaltney

CLAYTON, JAMES and ELIZABETH UZZELL   October 11, 1793
    Surety, Seth Hunter

CLEMENTS, GEORGE and CHARLOTTE MARSHALL   November 25, 1795
    Surety, Francis Young

COCKE, RICHARD H. and CHARLOTTE MACKIE   October 15, 1798
    Surety, Francis Young

COCKE, WILLIAM and ELIZABETH MACKIE   December 4, 1793
    Surety, Robert Taylor
    Parent, Martha Mackie

COGGAN, HENRY and ELIZABETH BRIGGS   December 3, 1792
    Surety, William Carstaphen

COOK, JOHN and RACHEL GREEN   February 21, 1795
    Surety, William Green

COOK, ROBERT NEWTON and ELIZABETH NORSEWORTHY July 24, 1792
    Surety, Andrew Bryan

COPELAND, ISHAM and CHARLOTTE FULGHAM   February 17, 1792
    Surety, Ralph West
    Consent of George Benn

CORBELL, RICHARD and ADA STOAKLEY   March 31, 1796
    Surety, Scarsbrook Godwin
    Guardian, Ismiah Pitt

CORBELL, WILLIS and NANCY JARVIS   November 5, 1788
    Surety, Ismiah Pitt
    Witness, Betsey Pitt

CORBETT, JOHNSON and ELIZABETH COFFIELD   November 27, 1783
    Surety, William Inglish
    Consent of Elizabeth Coffield,
    Samuel Corbett and Jule Corbett

CORNWELL, WILLIAM and DIANA MOODY   August 3, 1795
    Surety, Joseph Moody
    Witness, James Young

COUNCIL, JOSHUA and PEGGY BERKLEY (BUNKLEY) September 30, 1793
    Surety, Benjamin Eley

COUNCIL, MILES and ELIZABETH ELEY   May 28, 1784
    Parent, Robert Eley

CROCKER, DRURY and LUCY BARLOW
      Surety, Benjamin Hicks
      Consent of Anthony Crocker and
      George Barlow

February 12, 1793

CROCKER, MILNER and MARY CHAPMAN
      Surety, Samuel Woodley
      Parent, Benjamin Chapman

February 4, 1800

CROCKER, WILLIAM and ELIZABETH ALLEN
      Surety, James Wills

February 4, 1790

CRUMPLER, JOHN and BETSEY MARSHALL
      Surety, James Holland
      Consent of Dempsey Marshall

February 3, 1790

CUTCHIN, JOSIAH and ANN HALL
      Parent, Thomas Hall

June 30, 1787

DANIEL, ELIAS and PATSEY COGGAN
      Surety, Hardy Chapman

January 2, 1792

DANIEL, GILES and MARY JORDAN
      Surety, Joseph Godwin
      Witness, Thomas Hall

January 12, 1790

DANIEL, MILLS and MARY WHITEHEAD
      Surety, Jesse Whitehead
      Mother of Mary, Elizabeth Britt

December 17, 1787

DARBY, GEORGE and JULIANA WILLIAMS
      Surety, Henry Bain

October 2, 1798

DARDEN, DEMPSEY and POLLY SWANN ELEY
      Surety, Henry Saunders
      Parent, Robert Eley

March 2, 1793

DARDEN, JOHN and PATIENCE WATKINS
      Surety, John Watkins

August 7, 1788

DARDEN, JOHN JR. and ELIZABETH HOLLAND
      Surety, John Darden, son of Hardy
      Consent of Benjamin Holland

April 9, 1788

DARDEN, MILLS and PAMELIA LAWRENCE
      Surety, James Wills
      Consent of Mills Lawrence

July 18, 1795

DARDEN, THOMAS and BARSHEBA WILLS
      Surety, Miles Wills Jr.
      Parent, John Scarsbrook Wills

January 7, 1792

DAUGHTREY, DAVID and AGATHA COUNCIL
      Surety, Amos Council
      Parent, Scutchins Council

February 10, 1787

DAUGHTREY, ELISHA and SALLY DUCK
      Surety, John Duck

January 27, 1791

DAVIS, DARDEN and ELIZABETH CARR
      Surety, Joseph Atkins

January 24, 1798

DAVIS, JAMES and MARY HADLEY

February 1, 1778

Surety, Benjamin Chapman
Parent, Ambrose Hadley

DAVIS, JOHN and MARY UZZELL   September 14, 1791
      Surety, Edward Davis

DAVIS, JOSIAH and POLLY THOMAS   December 21, 1790
      Surety, James Wills

DAVIS, WILLIAM and CATEY WHITFIELD (widow)   February 7, 1783
      Surety, Richard Hardy

DEWS, THOMAS and CHARLOTTE WOMBWELL   January 9, 1792
      Surety, William Wombwell
      Parent, Britton Wombwell

DICKINSON, JACOB and MILLIE RICHARDS   November 16, 1772
      Surety, Miles Wills
      Witness, Emanuel Wills and
      William Bailey Jr.

DICKINSON, JACOB and MARY WHITFIELD   December 3, 1791
      Surety, Edmond Godwin
      Witness, Francis Young Jr.

DIGGES, COLE and MARY ROBINSON PURDIE   June 10, 1784
      Surety, Sampson Wilson
      Witness, Francis Wills

DIXON, MURPHY and LYDIA HAIL   April 2, 1792
      Surety, Horatio Green

DIXON, WILLIAM and ELIZABETH POPE   December 27, 1790
      Surety, Joseph Everett

DOBBS, JOHN and CATY JAMES   October 12, 1797
      Surety, James Pyland and
      John Shelly

DOWTY, ADDISON and ELIZABETH PITMAN   January 27, 1791
      Surety, Josiah Bidgood

DREW, DOLPHIN and PEGGY JORDAN   January 1, 1791
      Consent of Richard Jordan

DRIVER, JOSEPH and PRISCILLA WHITFIELD   January 26, 1790
      Surety, Richard Williams
      Witness, Edmond Mason

DUCK, JOSIAH and SARAH HOUSE   January 2, 1792
      Surety, George Lankford

DUCK, WILLIAM and HOLLAND DUCK   January 7, 1790
      Surety, Mills Carr

DUFF, WILLIAM and ANN WRIGHT   April 13, 1792
      Surety, Bennett Young

DUGGIN, JOSHUA and SALLY JOLLIFF   January 21, 1790
      Surety, Samuel Smith
      Witness, Lemuel Lightfoot

EDWARD, JOHN and ANNA COPHER   March 5, 1798
    Surety, James Gwaltney, guardian
    of Anna Copher

EDWARDS, DAVIS and CHLOETE CHAPMAN   December 22, 1790
    Surety, Wiggs Chapman
    Parent, John Chapman Sr.
    Witness, Francis Young

EDWARDS, GEORGE and ELIZABETH SMITH   June 27, 1795
    Surety, Robert Nicolson
    Witness, William Hamilton

EDWARDS, HENRY and NANCY HARRISON   April 2, 1792
    Surety, Patrick Gwaltney

EDWARDS, J'ANSON and SALLY HARDY   February 1, 1796
    Surety, Joseph Stallings

EDWARDS, SHELTON and ANGELINA GRAY   January 4, 1792
    Surety, Benjamin Ward

ELEY, JOHN and HONOUR BEAL   May 3, 1790
    Surety, Robert Beal

ELEY, JOHN and SALLY WATKINS   November 24, 1792
    Surety, Mills Eley
    Consent of Robert Watkins

ELEY, ROBERT and JEMIMA JOHNSON   April 15, 1784
    Surety, John Darden
    Witness, Francis Young
    Parents, Elizabeth and Michael Johnson

ELLSBERRY, THOMAS and MARTH POWELL   November 12, 1796
    Surety, Henry Pruden

ENGLISH, JOHN and PRISCILLA COFFIELD   September 6, 1787
    Surety, John English

EVERETT, MICHAEL and PEGGY JORDAN COWLING   January 7, 1790
    Surety, Thomas Cowling
    Witness, Francis Young

EVERETT, THOMAS and MARTHA WILLS   May 24, 1783
    Parent, Miles Wills
    Witness, Francis Young Jr.

EVERETT, THOMAS and ------ MATTHEWS   November 20, 1800
    Surety, John Giles
    Parent, Joseph Mathis (Matthews)

FARROW, JOHN and TABITHA BROWN   April 10, 1792
    Surety, John Brown

FIFE, MALLACHI and MARY HAWKINS   December 4, 1788
    Surety, Samuel Holladay

FITZPATRICK, FARROW and ELIZABETH BROCK   November 2, 1773
    Surety, Joseph Chapman

FLETCHER, JAMES and NANCY SEGAR   April 14, 1798
    Surety, William Segar

FLINT, THOMAS and ELIZABETH GODWIN   February 17, 1792
     Surety, Robert Nicholson
     Parent, Silvia Godwin

FLOOD, THOMAS and ELIZABETH GALE   January 9, 1787
     Surety, Edward Davis

FOWLER, JAMES and MOURNING CARR   December 10, 1787
     Surety, Samuel Fowler

FULGHAM, JEREMIAH and ELIZABETH GRAY   May 5, 1788
     Surety, Hugh Montgomery
     Witness, Samuel and John Womble

FULGHAM, JOHN and HOLLAND JONES   May 1, 1797
     Witness, Samuel Britt

FULGHAM, MATHEW and REBECCA WESTRAY   February 5, 1793
     Surety, Jeremiah Westray

GABRIEL, JOHN FRANCIS and PAMELIA SMITH   April 3, 1787
     Surety, Thomas Pierce

GALE, JOHN and CHLOE BABB   September 27, 1783
     Surety, William Baldwin, father-in-law
     of Chloe Babb

GALE, THOMAS and CHLOE FATHERLIE   September 6, 1790
     Surety, Joseph Everett

GALE, THOMAS and PATSEY GALE   January 2, 1795
     Surety, Henry Pruden

GALE, THOMAS and PEGGY SPENCER   May 26, 1800
     Surety, Samuel Everett
     Witness, Jethro Gale and Henry
     Saunders

GALE, THOMAS WHITNEY and SARAH DAVIS (widow) February 1, 1787
     Surety, Edward Davis

GARNER, JAMES and SALLY PARNALL   December 21, 1792
     Surety, Willis Parnall

GARNER, JOSEPH and SALLY AL-----   December 22, 1797
     Surety, William Allmond

GARNER, MATHEW and ELIZABETH DAUGHTRY (widow) November 29, 1783
     Surety, James Vaughan
     Witness, Francis Young

GARNER, MATHEW and PEGGY VAUGHAN   February 20, 1796
     Surety, Mathew Daughtry
     Parent, Adah and Uriah Vaughan

GARNER, THOMAS and MARY HALL   January 5, 1787
     Surety, Jonas Askew

GARTON, WILLIAM and MARY HODSDEN   January 20, 1793
     Surety, William Malcolm

GARTON, WILLIAM and ----------   August 12, 1797
     Surety, Richard Taylor

66

GASKINS, THOMAS and MILLY FULGHAM   November 15, 1787
     Surety, Henry Fulgham

GAY, ALLEN and ELIZABETH POWELL   January 5, 1793
     Parent, William Powell

GAY, EVERETT and SUSANNA BEST   January 30, 1796
     Surety, Richard Chapman

GIBBS, GABRIEL and ELIZABETH WILLS (widow) February 15, 1798
     Surety, James Barlow

GIBBS, JOHN and POLLY DRIVER   December 8, 1791
     Surety, Dolphin Driver
     Parent, Robert Driver

GILES, JOHN and TABITHA PINNER   August 1, 1796
     Surety, Barnaby Beal

GODFREY, WILLIAM and PATSEY NEWMAN   December 6, 1792
     Parent, Thomas Newman

GODWIN, EDMUND and HOLLAND WILLS   September 19, 1788
     Surety, Francis Young
     Parent, John Scarsbrook Wills

GODWIN, EDMUND and SUSANNA GRAY   May 2, 1800
     Surety, William Bagnall
     Parent, Elizabeth Gray

GODWIN, ELISHA and ELIZABETH STOAKLEY   July 28, 1795
     Surety, Robert R. Read
     Guardian, Ishmiah Pitt

GODWIN, GEORGE and PAMELIA POPE   December 19, 1795
     Surety, Joseph Godwin
     Parent, Sweeting Pope

GODWIN, JAMES and ELIZABETH GODWIN   September 15, 1796
     Surety, Burgh Godwin
     Guardian, Roland Reynolds

GODWIN, JONATHAN and PATSEY HOLLADAY   April 30, 1800
     Surety, Stephen Smith

GODWIN, JOSEPH and LETITIA WILLIAMS   September 6, 1790
     Surety, Josiah Cutchins

GODWIN, JOSEPH and NANCY SMITH   September 14, 1795
     Surety, William Rand Smith
     Guardian, James Pitt

GODWIN, WILLIAM and PATSEY BUNKLEY   August 9, 1800
     Surety, Richard Williams
     Parent, Sally Bunkley

GODWIN, WILLIS and SALLY DANIEL   July 14, 1798
     Surety, Giles Daniel

GODWIN, WRIGHT and POLLY GODWIN   February 27, 1793
     Surety, Robert R. Read
     Guardian, Roland Reynolds

GOODRICH, GEORGE and NANCY TURNER   October 19, 1792
     Surety, William Goodrich
     Parent, Martha Turner

```
GOODRICH, WILLIAM and POLLY DUGGIN          March 24, 1792
     Surety, Joshua Duggin

GOODSON, NICHOLAS and ELIZABETH BULLOCK     December 20, 1792
     Surety, John Goodson

GOODSON, WILLIS and PEGGY MOORE             August 23, 1798
     Surety, Nicholas Goodson

GRAY, JAMES and ESTHER PITT                 March 1, 1798
     Surety, Francis Young
     Parent, Elizabeth Pitt

GRAY, JAMES and SALLY GODWIN WILLS          December 17,1791
     Surety, Miles Wills
     Witness, Edmund Mason

GRAY, JESSE and MARTHA DAVIS                December 20, 1787
     Surety, John J. Wheadon

GRAY, JOSEPH and SALLY MISTER               March 7, 1791
     Surety, Josiah Applewhaite

GRAY, JOSEPH and FRANCES WHITE              May 7, 1792
     Surety, William Waltham

GRAY, JOSIAH and MARTH EVERETT (widow)      October 21, 1791
     Surety, Miles Wills

GRAY, NATHANIEL and LYDIA DRIVER            October 7, 1790
     Surety, Ralph West
     Consent of James Morrison
     Witness, Edmund Mason

GRAY, SAMUEL and MARY MANGAM                January 22, 1790
     Surety, Richard Mangam
     Parent, Micajah Mangam
     Witness, Edmund Mason and
     Francis Young Jr.

GRAY, WILLIS and FRANCES CROCKER            January 23, 1796
     Surety, Joseph Parnall, father-in-law
     of Frances

GRAYHAM, THOMAS and SARAH BARMER            August 23, 1792
     Surety, Edward Brown

GREEN, HORATIO and MARY HOWELL              January 26, 1788
     Surety, Samuel Bradley

GROCE, CHARLES and SALLY SMELLY             August 19, 1790
     Surety, Josiah Davis

GROCE, WILLIAM and SARAH FRIZZELL           August 31, 1787
     Surety, Ralph West

GWALTNEY, SIMMONS and SALLY HOLLEMAN        April 1, 1793
     Surety, Jesse Holleman

GWIN, SOLOMON and HONOUR DUCK               November 6, 1796
     Surety, Thomas Johnson
     Witness, Abraham Carr
```

HAILE, THOMAS and MARY DAVIS   March --, 1787
    Surety, Michael Norsworthy

HALL, GEORGE and PRISCILLA GARNER   November 7, 1796
    Surety, Thomas Garner

HALL, ISAAC and ELIZABETH QUAY (widow)   May 23, 1795
    Surety, John Jordan

HALL, THOMAS and ELIZABETH GOODSON (widow)   February 6, 1796
    Surety, John Hall

HAMILTON, WILLIAM and LUCY LEE   July 17, 1784
    Surety, Stephen Garton
    Witness, David and Francis Young Jr.

HAMPTON, ELIJAH and CHLOE HOWELL   April 28, 1795
    Surety, Samuel Everett
    Witness, Samuel Hampton

HAMPTON, SAMUEL and PATSEY HOWELL   July 19, 1790
    Surety, James Beal

HANCOCK, JOHN and NANCY WILLIAMS   May 16, 1793
    Surety, Thomas Hancock
    Parent, Richard Williams

HARDY, WILLIAM and SARAH DERRING (widow)   December 18, 1792
    Surety, ----- Young

HARRIS, JAMES and SALLY WESTRAY   December 22, 1797
    Surety, Mills Westray

HARRIS, WILLIAM and SWEETING DUKE   October 24, 1788
    Surety, Joseph Clark
    Witness, Francis Young Jr.

HARRIS, WILLIAM and MARY JORDAN   September 20, 1790
    Surety, John Chapman
    Witness, John Hancock

HARRISON, HENRY and ELIZABETH CASEY   July 14, 1798
    Surety, Thomas Casey

HARRISON, JOHN and NANCY JORDAN   January 2, 1784
    Surety, James Young
    Parent, Martha Jordan

HART, EDWIN and ELIZABETH DAUGHTREY   May 11, 1796
    Surety, James Johnston

HARVEY, JAMES and SALLY GODFREY   August 20, 1793
    Surety, Charles Godfrey
    Parent, Lemuel Godfrey

HATCHELL, WILLIAM and HOLLAND LAWRENCE   December 6, 1787
    Surety, Nathaniel Vellines

HAWKINS, SAMUEL and SALLY PARKER   June 27, 1783
    Surety, Joseph Parker
    Parent, Thomas Parker
    Witness, Benjamin Hawkins and Francis Young

HEATH, ISAIAH and REBECCA UZZELL   May 5, 1795
    Surety, Thomas Joyner

HEATH, ROBERT and ROSEY DOWTY   September 3, 1793
        Surety, James Pyland

HEDGPETH, ELISHA and CHASTY DUCK   September 21, 1793
        Surety, Charles Roundtree
        Consent of John Duck and wife Mary,
        and Henry Hedgpeth and wife Elizabeth
        Witness, Elisha Owen

HERRING, DANIEL and HANNAH HARDY   January 24, 1793
        Surety, George Hardy

HILTON, JOHN and PEGGY ROBERTSON   March 26, 1791
        Surety, Patrick Ronaldson

HOBBS, PETER and CHARLOTTE McCOY   January 18, 1787
        Surety, Samuel McCoy

HOCKADAY, JOHN and MARY ORR   January 23, 1793
        Surety, Francis Young Jr.
        Witness, Thomas Pierce

HOLLADAY, ANTHONY and ANN GODFREY   June 8, 1787
        Surety, Francis Young
        Parent, Samuel Godfrey

HOLLADAY, HEZEKIAH and PRUDENCE WILLIAMS (widow)
        Surety, Thomas Hancock   December 13, 1796

HOLLADAY, JOSIAH and MARTHA DANIEL   December 24, 1792
        Surety, Giles Daniel

HOLLADAY, MILLS and MARTHA WRENN   November 2, 1791
        Surety, James Young

HOLLADAY, SAMUEL and MARY HARVEY   December 18, 1797
        Surety, Hezekiah Holladay,
        father-in-law of Mary

HOLLADAY, THOMAS and TEMPY BRIDGER   January 5, 1795
        Surety, Elias Herring
        Guardian, Simon Boykin
        Witness, J. S. Bridger

HOLLAND, JACOB and TEMPY JOHNSON   February 15, 1800
        Surety, Eley Johnson

HOLLAND, JAMES and POLLY HARRIS   October 16, 1790
        Surety, Lewis Harris
        Witness, Peyton Young

HOLLAND, JOHN and MILLA ROBERTS   March 16, 1796
        Surety, John Saunders

HOLLEMAN, ARTHUR and SALLY APPLEWHAITE   April 30, 1800
        Surety, Francis Young
        James Atkinson, guardian to Sally

HOLLEMAN, JOHN and NANCY THOMAS   December 5, 1791
        Surety, Phillip Thomas
        Parent, John Thomas
        Witness, Jesse Thomas

HOLMES, JOSEPH and MARY LAWRENCE (widow)   August 5, 1793
        Surety, James Johnson
        Witness, E. Mason

HOLSFORD, WILLIS and ELIZABETH WHITLEY   March 28, 1793
    Surety, Joseph Moody

HOWARD, HENRY and ELIZABETH WHITLEY   December 6, 1798
    Surety, Francis Young

HUNTER, SETH and ELIZABETH -----   February 11, 1791
    Surety, John Provan

HUTCHINSON, JOHN and PEGGY JAMES (widow)   July 3, 1793
    Surety, John Broadfield

INGLISH, JESSE and MARTHA WATKINS   March 18, 1793
    Surety, JOhn Inglish

INGLISH, THOMAS and HOLLAND DUCK   November 7, 1796
    Surety, Thomas Johnson

JACOBS, THOMAS and ANN MARY PITT   October 13, 1788
    Surety, Abel James Jr.

JAMES, ABEL JR. and CORNELIA KEPPS   October 13, 1788
    Surety, Thomas Jacobs

JAMES, ELIAS and CITTEY NORSWORTHY   July 4, 1783

JEFFERSON, SAMUEL and TEMPERANCE WOMBWELL   October 5, 1795
    Surety, Thomas Dews
    Parent, Britton Wombwell

JEMACIA, HENRY and KEZIAH GARNER   December 29, 1796
    Surety, James Garner

JOHNSON, JACOB and PATIENCE HOLLAND   November 17, 1796
    Surety, Eley Johnson

JOHNSON, JAMES and MARY CHAPPELL   January 7, 1790
    Surety, Francis Vaughan
    Witness, Peyton Young

JOHNSON, JOHN and MARY LANKFORD   April 5, 1787
    Surety, Amos Johnson
    Witness, Francis Young

JOHNSON, JOHN and ANN ATKINS (widow)   April 12, 1788
    Surety, George Clayton

JOHNSON, JOHN and ANN BIDGOOD   November 19, 1791
    Surety, Joshua Duggin
    Witness, Edmund Mason

JOHNSON, JORDAN and MARGARET ELEY   February 13, 1787
    Surety, Eley Johnson

JOHNSON, JORDAN and HOLLAND -----   February 6, 1797
    Surety, Joseph B------

JOHNSON, MATHEW and PATIENCE ELEY   February 5, 1793
    Surety, James Tomlin
    Parent, William Eley

71

JOHNSON, WILLIAM and MOORE TAYLOR Surety, John Nelms	January 11, 1791
JOHNSON, WILLIS and LILLEY BUTLER Benjamin Bradshaw	August 7, 1788
JOHNSTON, JAMES and ELIZABETH SMITH Parent, Thomas Smith	September 19, 1798
JOLIFF, SCARSBROOK and SARAH TARLETON Surety, Samuel Smith	November 19, 1788
JONES, ABAHAM and NANCY WARD Surety, William Stringfield	October 30, 1798
JONES, ALLEN and JEMIAH JOHNSON	March 31, 1798
JONES, BENJAMIN JR. and ANN WARD (widow) Surety, Thomas Wrenn	March 25, 1783
JONES, DAVIS and CLARA BANKS Surety, Francis Young	June 5, 1795
JONES, HENRY and SALLY DAVIS Surety, Joseph Carrell	April 7, 1800
JONES, NATHANIEL and PRISCILLA FONES Surety, Benjamin Goodrich	July 5, 1787
JONES, NATHANIEL and POLLY DAVIS Surety, Jesse Gray	December 31, 1796
JONES, PERSON and ELIZABETH JONES Surety, Nathaniel Jones	March 7, 1793
JONES, THOMAS and POLLY PATTERSON Surety, George Gray Consent of William Patterson	July 7, 1800
JONES, WILLIAM and MARTHA NORSWORTHY Surety, Simmons Gwaltney	July 2, 1792
JORDAN, NICHOLAS and CHARLOTTE CHAPMAN Surety, Wilson Davis	July 7, 1798
JORDAN, ROBERT and PEGGY JORDAN Surety, Thomas Jordan	April 3, 1797
JORDAN, WILLIAM and SALLY TYNES Surety, Francis Young	February 24, 1784
JORDAN, WILLIAM and MARY PERSON Surety, Britton Womble Witness, Sylvia West	April 22, 1788
JORDAN, WILLIAM and MARTHA MARSHALL Surety, Pleasant and Thomas Jordan	February 1, 1796
JORDAN, WILLIAM and MARTHA BIDGOOD Surety, Micajah Bidgood	December 22, 1797

KELLY, MICHAEL and SALLY BRASWELL   March 29, 1791
    Surety, Francis Young

KIMBALL, JOHN and JENNY SMITH   December 15, 1796
    Surety, Henry Turner

KING, JOHN and FANNY WHITFIELD   January 15, 1798
    Surety, Joseph Driver

LANKFORD, WILEY and WINNEY POPE   September 6, 1790
    Surety, John Watkins

LAWRENCE, GEORGE and SALLY BEAL   January 13, 1792
    Surety, James Beal

LAWRENCE, JOHN and MARY BRIDGER   January 13, 1773
    Surety, James Bridger
    Witness, William Bailey

LAWRENCE, JOHN and POLLY OUTLAND   January 5, 1791
    Surety, James Howell

LEVY, LAZRUS and SARAH DRUMMOND (widow)   May 22, 1795
    Surety, Francis Young

LOWRY, ISAAC and JANE ABBINGTON   October 26, 1787
    Surety, James Davis

MAGET, WILLIAM and PRISCILLA HARDY   June 24, 1795
    Surety, Robert Hunnicutt

MAHONE, WILLIAM and WILMUTH WOMBLE   February 18, 1797
    Surety, Micajah Munford
    Parent, Harty Womble
    Witness, Nancy Bond

MALLICOTE, THOMAS and MILLY LUPO   August 7, 1790
    Surety, John Harrison
    Witness, Peyton Young

MALLORY, WILLIAM and MARY BRYAN   July 20, 1792
    Surety, Francis Young Jr.
    Guardian, Solomon Pace of
    Northampton County, N. C.

MANGAM, JOSIAH and ELIZABETH ABBITT   September 20, 1791
    Surety, Dolphin Davis

MARSHALL, JOHN JR. and TEMPERANCE COPELAND October 30, 1772
    Surety, John Marshall

MARTIN, JAMES and POLLY BAGNALL   December 8, 1796
    Surety, John Lawrence

MASON, EDMUND and FRANCIS YOUNG   February 17, 1792
    Parent, Francis Young

MATTHEWS, BENJAMIN and TEMPY NEAVILL   April 21, 1791
    Surety, Joseph Everitt

MATTHEWS, JAMES and ANN BRANTLEY   December 12, 1788
    Surety, Francis Young

```
MATTHEWS, JOHN and MARY DAVIS              September 13, 1793
    Surety, John Davis

MATTHEWS, KINCHEN and NANCY EDWARDS        December 7, 1798
    Surety, John Davis

MATTHEWS, RICHARD and ELIZABETH PARR       March 31, 1790
    Surety, Joseph Shivers
    Witness, Jesse Mathews

MEARS, RICHARD and CHRISTIAN NORSWORTHY (widow)
    Surety, William Walden                 August 4, 1784

MERCER, JAMES and PATIENCE FULGHAM (widow) October 1, 1792
    Surety, Jesse Fulgham

MILNER, MILLS and LUCY PHILLIPS            March 21, 1792
    Surety, Benjamin Phillips
    Parent, John Phillips

MINIARD, JOSEPH and AMELIA CUTCHINS        June 2, 1792
    Surety, Thomas Wills

MINYARD, JOSEPH and CHARLOTTE NORSWORTHY   January 17, 1788
    Surety, Charles Groce
    Witness, John Godwin

MOODY, ISHMAEL and SARAH BRANTLEY          August 8, 1787
    Surety, Francis Young
    Parent, Wilson Brantley

MOODY, WILLIAM and FANNY FATHERLIE         May 20, 1790
    Surety, John Moody
    Witness, Edward Davis

MOORE, AARON and PATSEY TUCKER             February 3, 1796
    Surety, William Carrell
    Aaron Moore of Surry County

MORRIS, JAMES and SWEETING DUKE            December 27, 1791
    Surety, Isham Davis

MORRIS, WILLIAM and ANN WILSON             May 2, 1795
    Surety, William Allen

MOUNTFORD, THOMAS and NANCY SHELLY         February 8, 1791

MURPHREY, CHARLES and POLLY MOODY          March 6, 1790
    Surety, Joseph Moody

MURPHREY, JESSE and LOISA CUTCHINS         August 5, 1793
    Surety, Ralph West
    Witness, Edmund Mason

MURPHY, DEMPSEY and RACHEL NELMS           October 19, 1790
    Surety, John Murphy

MURRY, JAMES and CHARLOTTE BAGNALL         May 6, 1793
    Surety, John Clark
    Parent, Mary Holladay
    Witness, Peyton Young

MURRY, JAMES and BETSEY PROCTOR            December 26, 1797
    Surety, William Proctor
```

McCLINCHEY, THOMAS and NANCY BOWDEN   January 26, 1791
   Surety, Richard Bowden

McCLOUD, NORMAN and PATTEY MURRY   April 18, 1788
   Parent, John Milner
   Witness, Joseph Stallings and
   Patrick Braddy

McCOY, ADAM and SARAH JOLLY   March 15, 1793
   Surety, Samuel McCoy
   Parent, John Jolly

McDONALD, PHILLIP and MARY SULLIVAN   July 20, 1792
   Surety, Francis Young Jr.

McWILLIAMS, THOMAS and HOLLAND PARKER   April 30, 1784
   Surety, Josiah Parker
   Parent, Nicholas Parker
   Witness, Francis Young

McWILLIAMS, THOMAS and JENNY HUBARD   May 24, 1791
   Parent, William Hubbard

NELMS, JOHN and ANN COFIELD   February 2, 1790
   Surety, Josiah Duck
   Parent, Julia Corbett

NELSON, JOHN and POLLY MILLER   December 5, 1791
   Surety, Sampson Barlow
   Wilson Whitfield, father-in-law
   to Polly Miller

NELSON, WILLIAM and TABITHA ENGLISH   February 7, 1791
   Surety, John Pierce

NEWMAN, SOLOMON and LYDIA JONES   May 24, 1791
   Surety, Thomas Garner
   Parent, Mary Jones
   Witness, James Garner

NICHOLSON, ROBERT and MARY BUTLER (widow)   February 7, 1788
   Surety, Charles Groce

NORSWORTHY, JOHN and JENNY OUTLAND   January 26, 1773
   Surety, George Norsworthy
   Witness, William Bailey

NORSEWORTHY, JOSEPH and LYDIA CHAPMAN   January 13, 1800
   Surety, Stephen Smith

NORSWORTHY, THOMPSON and POLLY CUTCHIN   September 11, 1800
   Surety, Dolphin Driver

OUTLAND, THOMAS and NANCY BABB   February 19, 1800
   Surety, Andrew Woodley

OUTLAND, WILLIAM JR. and REBECCA STRINGFIELD December 16, 1788
   Surety, Joseph Stringfield
   Parent, James Stringfield

PARKER, HARDY and ELIZABETH CARR. Parent, John Carr	February 6, 1791
PARKER, JOSEPH and MARY HUTCHINGS Surety, Thomas Hall	February 13, 1793
PARKER, JOSIAH (Merchant) and MARY BRIDGER, widow of Col. Jos. Bridger Surety, Daniel Herring Witness, William Bailey Jr.	May 26, 1773
PARKER, WILLIAM and MARTHA BREWER (widow) Surety, Benjamin Holland	January 3, 1787
PARKINSON, JACOB and HOLLAND SMITH Surety, John Smith	Febraury 13, 1790
PARR, JOHN and BETSEY DANIEL Surety, John Daniel	April 29, 1800
PARR, RICHARD and POLLY HEATH Surety, Isaiah Heath	May 4, 1796
PARR, RICHARD and NANCY MATTHEWS Surety, Joseph Shivers	January 15, 1800
PARR, WILLIAM and FLORENTINE CALLCOTE Surety, David Bradley	October 26, 1796
PATRICK, WILLIAM and MARGARET EASSON Surety, John Easson	June 3, 1791
PEIRCE, JOHN and SALLY JOHNSON Surety, William Nelms	February 7, 1791
PEIRCE, JOHN and MILDRED JOYNER Surety, Thomas Davis Witness, Darden Davis	February 5, 1796
PEIRCE, RICHARD and POLLY WRENN Surety, Josiah Wrenn	December 26, 1795
PERSON, WILLIAM and FRANCES JORDAN Surety, James Barlow	June 2, 1800
PETTIT, GEORGE and NANCY BARLOW Surety, William Fisher Parent, James Barlow Witness, Francis and Bennett Young	October 20, 1787
PHILLIPS, BENJAMIN and HOLLAND EDWARDS Surety, Joel Phillips Francis Boykin, guardian of Benjamin Phillips	August 8, 1796
PINHORN, JOHN and MARY UZZELL Surety, Thomas Uzzell	December 18, 1788
PITMAN, AARON and CREASY JONES Surety, Sampson Harrison	April 17, 1790
PITMAN, THOMAS and LUCKY WOMBWELL Surety, Peter Vaniser	March 4, 1796
PITT, JOHN and ANN SMITH Surety, John Pasteur	July 20, 1784

76

```
PITT, JOSEPH and JENNETT NEWMAN              March 7, 1796
     Surety, Jesse Matthews

PITT, ISHMIAH and BETSEY STOKLEY             November 29, 1787
     Surety, John Reynolds

PITT, PURNELL and SARAH BUTLER               June 29, 1796
     Surety, Thomas Hancock
     Parent, John Butler, decd.
     Guardian, Josiah Wills

POPE, JOHN and PEGGY GOODSON                 ---------, 1794
     Parent, James and Elley Goodson
     Witness, Nathaniel Young

POPE, ROBERT and ELIZABETH GILES             June 25, 1793
     Surety, William Dixon
     Consent of John Giles

POWELL, BENJAMIN and MARY GAY                March 10, 1792
     Parent, William Gay

POWELL, GEORGE and MARTHA BATTEN (widow)     February 4, 1790
     Surety, John Powell

POWELL, GIDEON and MARY ASKEW                June 30, 1798
     Surety, SAmuel Everitt

POWELL, MATHEW and MILLY DANIEL              March 5, 1791
     Surety, William Gay
     Witness, Edmund Mason

POWELL, SAMUEL and SALLY WESTRAY (widow)     January 14, 1792
     Surety, Hardy Chapman

POWELL, SEYMORE and SALLY BRIGGS             April 25, 1793
     Surety, David Briggs

POWELL, THADEUS and MARY POWELL              October 6, 1793
     Surety, Allen Johnson

PROVANS, JOHN and BETSEY HOLLADAY PARR       April 7, 1791
     Surety, William Parr
     Witness, Francis Young Jr.

PRUDEN, HENRY and MILDRED MILNER             July 3, 1783
     Surety, Jacob Dickinson
     Witness, Francis Young

PRUDEN, JOHN and MOURNING ------             -------7, 1800
     Surety, John Watkins


QUAY, SAMUEL and BETSEY GIBBS (widow)        May 1, 1783
     Surety, John Bridger


RAND, WALTER and MARY PARKER                 February 6, 1783
     Surety, Elias Parker
     Witness, Francis Young

RED, JOSIAH and PRISCILLA INGLISH            December 9, 1788
     Surety, John Darden Jr.
     Consent of Patience Inglish
```

REYNOLDS, JOHN and ELIZABETH WHITLEY.   January 13, 1792
        Surety, Charles Groce
        Parent, Tabitha Whitley

REYNOLDS, JOHN and POLLY JORDAN   November 17, 1798
        Surety, Richard Reynolds
        Parent, Betsey Jordan

REYNOLDS, RANDALL and MARTHA DICKINSON   November 9, 1795
        Surety, Charles Groce

REYNOLDS, ROWLAND and MARTHA GODWIN   July 3, 1787
        Surety, John Reynolds
        Martha the widow of Jeremiah Godwin

RIDER, THOMAS and COURTNEY JONES   March 6, 1787
        Surety, William Hamilton

ROBERTS, EDWIN and POLLY JONES   January 7, 1796
        Surety, Thomas Jones

ROBERTS, WILLIS and MARY RHODES   April 8, 1800
        Surety, John Holland

ROBERTSON, JOSEPH R. and NANCY LAWRENCE   February 1, 1783
        Surety, Miles Lawrence
        Parent, Elizabeth Lawrence
        Witness, Francis Young and Thomas Inglish

ROSS, JOHN and CHARLOTTE DURLEY   December 12, 1773
        Surety, Henry Pitt
        Parent or guardian, Horatio Durley
        Witness, Sarah Durley

ROSS, JOHN and PATIENCE CARR   June 1, 1795
        Surety, Brewer Godwin

RUDKIN, WILLIAM and ELIZABETH STEVENS   October 7, 1793
        Surety, John Turner

SAMPSON, PETER and ROSE McGRIGORY (widow)   June 5, 1783
        Surety, Stephen Gordon
        Witness, Francis Young

SAMPSON, PETER and ANGELINA ATKINS   March 31, 1791
        Witness, George Purdie Jr.

SAUNDERS, BENJAMIN and ELIZABETH EDWARDS   January 25, 1796
        Surety, Joel Phillips
        Parent, Rebecca Edwards

SAUNDERS, JOHN and ANNE FLEMING (widow)   October 22, 1784
        Surety, Job Saunders

SAUNDERS, JOHN and HOLLAND BRITT   February 6, 1792
        Surety, John Coggan

SAUNDERS, THOMAS and ANNA JOHNSON   February 25, 1796
        Surety, John Saunders

SEWARD, WILLIAM and CHERRY PITMAN   October 19, 1795
        Surety, L'Anson Edwards

```
SHELLY, THOMAS and FRANCES EDWARDS              April 27, 1798
     Surety, Shelly White
     Parent, Martha Edwards

SHEPPERD, SAMUEL and MRS. PRUDENCE HARRISON    November 13, 1800
     Surety, Benjamin Weston

SHERROD, JOHN and TEMPERANCE SHIVERS           February 20, 1793
     Surety, William Shivers

SHIVERS, PETER and AMELIA HALLIFORD            January 4, 1787
     Surety, Campion Bracey

SMITH, JOSEPH and MARY RAND                    March 27, 1773
     Surety, Hezekiah Holladay
     Parent, Joseph Smith Sr. and
     Sophia Rand
     Witness, William Bailey Jr.

SMITH, JOSEPH and ANNE HOLLADAY                January 14, 1798
     Surety, William Bryant

SMITH, NICHOLAS and MARTHA HOUSE               March 29, 1791
     Surety, John Daniel

SMITH, SAMUEL and CONSTANT DAVIS (widow)       February 16, 1792
     Surety, Nicholas Smith

SMITH, SAMUEL and NANCY BOND (widow)           January 3, 1798
     Surety, Andrew Woodley

SMITH, SAMUEL and HOLLAND DAVIS                May 19, 1800
     Guardian, John Godwin

SMITH, STEPHEN and BETSEY GREEN GODWIN         December 6, 1787
     Surety, John Clark
     Parent, Samuel (Shamuel) Godwin

SMITH, THOMAS and ANN EDWARDS                  January 9, 1787
     Surety, Robert Edwards

SMITH, WILLIAM RAND and MARTHA NORSWORTHY      November 21, 1793
     Surety, James Pitt

SMITH, WILLIS and MARY APPLEWHAITE             November 1, 1797
     Surety, William Carter

STALLINGS, WILLIAM and MARY DAVIDSON           February 23, 1795
     Surety, Joseph Stallings
     Parent, Patty Davidson

STALLINGS, WILLIAM and MRS. PATSEY GRAY        April 7, 1800
     Surety, Gray Carrell

STEVENS, JOHN and HONOUR CARR                  September 6, 1790
     Surety, Wiley Lankford

STEVENS, JOHN and MARY MOUNTFORT               May 11, 1793
     Surety, Micajah Mountfort

STOTT, THOMAS and POLLY PITMAN                 October 1, 1795
     Surety, Addison Dowty

STRINGFIELD, WOMBLE and REBECCA JONES          February 13, 1797
     Surety, James Thomas
     Parent, Benjamin Jones
```

STROUD, JOHN and NANNY NORSWORTHY   November 6, 1788
    Surety, Thomas Gale
    Witness, Thomas Hail

STUCKEY, EDMUND and ELIZABETH RICHARDS   June 28, 1787
    Surety, Samuel McCoy
    Witness, Francis Young

TAYLOR, FREDERICK and ------- WOMBLE   January 16, 1792
    Parent, William Womble

TAYLOR, LUKE and BETHIAH CROCKER   September 6, 1787
    Surety, William Addison

TAYLOR, WILLIAM and NANCY LANCASTER   July 5, 1796
    Surety, William Barlow

THOMAS, JAMES and MOURNING MANGAM (widow)   June 30, 1795
    Surety, Benjamin Jones
    Residence Surry County

THOMAS, JORDAN and MARY HANCOCK   April 1, 1791
    Surety, Thomas Hancock
    Witness, Hardy Chapman

THOMPSON, HENRY and LUCY GILES   December 30, 1791
    Surety, Thomas Giles

THORNTON, WILLIAM and ELIZABETH WILLS   November 27, 1784
    Surety, Robert Tynes
    Consent of James Wills
    Witness, Francis Young Jr. and
    Francis Young Sr.

TOMLIN, ARTHUR and POLLY SIKES   February 9, 1796
    Surety, John Busby
    Parent, Andrew Sikes

TOMLIN, JOHN and CHARLOTTE HOLLAND   December 19, 1797
    Surety, Allen Johnson
    Parent, Joseph Holland

TURNER, HENRY and POLLY KIMBALL   November 24, 1796
    Surety, John Kimball

TURNER, JOHN and MARY LAWRENCE   June 6, 1791
    Surety, Joseph Britt
    Consent of Sawyer Lawrence

TURNER, MATHEW and ELIZABETH SAUNDERS   August 23, 1792
    Surety, Elias Saunders
    Parent, Sarah Saunders

TURNER, PEIRCE and BETTY POWELL   September 7, 1787
    Surety, Sion Boon
    Witness, Francis Young

TYNES, BENJAMIN and SUSANNA BRIDGER (widow) December 6, 1784
    Surety, James Allen Bridger

TYNES, BENJAMIN and ELIZABETH HILL   August 19, 1788
    Surety, Samuel Webb

TYNES, ROBERT and PATSEY GIBBS   December --, 1797

UNDERWOOD, THEOPHILUS and ----- JOYNER   February 8, 1784
      Surety, Richard Harrison
      Witness, Francis Young

UZZELL, THOMAS and POLLY JAMES (widow)   November 13, 1795
      Surety, Thomas King

VAUGHAN, JAMES and BETSEY COWLING   November 7, 1796
      Surety, Davis Cowling

VELLINES, ISAAC and SALLY MOODY   March 17, 1790
      Surety, William Blunt
      Witness, Betty Moody

WEEKS, JOHN and NANCY MOODY   March 13, 1798
      Joseph Moody, brother of Nancy
      Witness, Isaac Moody

WEBB, JAMES and ANN DRIVER   March 24, 1773
      Parent, Charles Driver
      Guardian, Samuel Webb
      Witness, William Watson and
      William Bailey Jr.

WESTON, BENJAMIN and CHARLOTTE GODWIN   May 23, 1793
      Surety, Thomas Flint
      Parent, Silvey Godwin
      Witness, Samuel Weston

WESTON, SAMUEL and RHODA BAINS   September 19, 1795
      Surety, Benjamin Weston
      Witness, Copeland Parker

WESTRAY, LEVI and SARAH TOMLIN   February 6, 1792
      Surety, John Tomlin
      Consent of Mathew and Elizabeth Tomlin

WESTRAY, SIMON and MARY SAUNDERS   May 28, 1787
      Surety, John Saunders
      Parent, Elizabeth Saunders

WHEELER, JACOB and NANCY ENGLISH   October 13, 1791
      Surety, William Nelms

WHITAKER, DUDLEY and POLLY WILLS   April 22, 1792
      Surety, Copeland Whitfield

WHITE, SHELLY and POLLY BROWN   March 16, 1792
      Surety, James Pyland

WHITE, WILLIAM and MARY HOLLEMAN   August 17, 1787
      Surety, Francis Young
      Witness, Edmund Mason

WHITEHEAD, JESSE and ESTHER MARSHALL   January 16, 1787
      Surety, Joshua Daniel

WHITFIELD, COPELAND JR. and PAMELIA WILLS   January 23, 1790
    Surety, Arthur Applewhaite
    Parent, Elvira Wills
    Witness, John Wills

WHITFIELD, COPELAND and CATHERINE HOWARD   February 19, 1791
    Surety, Francis Young Jr.

WHITFIELD, SAMUEL and FANNY NORSWORTHY   March 27, 1783
    Surety, Mills Norsworthy
    Parent, Tristram Norsworthy

WHITLEY, ISHMAEL and ELIZABETH McCOY (widow)   December 22, 1783
    Surety, Samuel Lightfoot
    Witness, Francis Young

WHITLEY, JOHN SAUNDERS and BARSHEBA BATEMAN   August 4, 1791
    Parent, Tabitha Whitley and
    John Bateman

WHITLEY, RANDALL and SARAH BRACEY   November 28, 1791
    Surety, Mills Whitley

WHITLEY, TIMOTHY and MARY JENKINS   October 12, 1787
    Surety, George Whitley

WHITLEY, WILLIAM and SALLY TURNER   July 6, 1790
    Surety, Thomas Turner

WILKINSON, COFER and MRS. JENNY LOWRY   April 8, 1800
    Surety, Simon Bland

WILKINSON, WILLIS and JANE CUTCHINS   June 3, 1784
    Surety, John Scarsbrook Wills

WILLIAMS, DAVID and PRUDENCE HARVEY (widow)   June --, 1787
    Surety, Willis Pitt

WILLIAMS, JORDAN and POLLY NORSWORTHY   November 17, 1798
    Guardian, Britten Britt

WILLIS, ROBERT and MARY RHODES   April 8, 1800

WILLS, JOSIAH and MARY DRIVER   December 30, 1772
    Parent, John Driver
    Witness, Randolph Whitley and
    James Wormeley

WILLS, JOSIAH and PATSEY UZZELL   December 11, 1797
    Surety, Bennett Young

WILLS, MATHEW and ELIZABETH NELSON (widow)   April 29, 1784
    Surety, Jesse Gray
    Witness, Francis Young

WILLS, NATHANIEL and MARY PEDEN   August 18, 1791
    Surety, John Wills
    Witness, Tristram Norsworthy

WILLS, THOMAS and ANN GRAY   November 5, 1793
    Surety, Nathaniel Gray

WILSON, GOODRICH and SALLY APPLEWHAITE LAWRENCE
    Surety, Joseph Holmes   November 2, 1798

WILSON, RANDALL and MILLY CHARITY   October 16, 1798
        Surety, Hartwell Charity

WILSON, ROBERT and ------ HUTCHINSON   April 15, 1793
        Parent, John Hutchinson

WILSON, SAMPSON and WINNEY BRANTLEY   July 4, 1791
        Surety, James Brantley
        Parent, Wilson Brantley

WILSON, SOLOMON and ANN RIDDICK   June 4, 1787
        Surety, Francis Young
        Witness, Edmund Mason

WOMBWELL, JEREMIAH and NANCY MOUNTFORT   December 28, 1792
        Surety, Micajah Mountfort
        Parent, Thomas Wombwell

WOMBWELL, JOHN and LUCY STALLINGS   January 1, 1802

WOMBWELL, LEMUEL and ANN DEFORD   February 17, 1790
        Surety, James Deford
        Parent, Ann Deford

WOMBWELL, THOMAS and NANCY OUTLAND   July 16, 1793
        Surety, William Outland

WOOD, JONOTHAN and MARTHA BOCOCK   November 7, 1797
        Parent, Peter Bocock

WOODLEY, ANDREW and ELIZABETH HILL HARRISON   November 7, 1797

WOODWARD, WILLIAM and TAMER COLE (widow)   December 25, 1787
        Surety, George Hall

WOOTEN, JOHN and ELIZABETH JORDAN   February 5, 1787
        Surety, Joseph Ellis

WRENN, FRANCIS and MARTHA HARRISON (widow)   January 18, 1774
        Surety, John Jordan, Jr.
        Witness, William Jordan and Francis Young

WRENN, FRANCIS and CATHERINE BROWN   May 21, 1800
        Surety, Richard Pierce
        Consent of John Mallicote

WRENN, JAMES and LUCY GWALTNEY   January 14, 1795
        Surety, James Gwaltney

WRENN, JOHN and PATIENCE CARRELL   April 13, 1787
        Surety, William Hardy
        Guardian, William Proctor
        Witness, Joseph Carrell and James Piland

WRIGHT, HENRY and REBECCA WATKINS   February 1, 1796
        Surety, Jesse Watkins

WRIGHT, MATHEW and SARAH BALDWIN   January 17, 1792
        Surety, William Goodrich

YOUNG, BENNETT and POLLY BENN GODWIN   March 22, 1792
        Surety, Edmund Mason
        Consent of George Benn
        Witness, Josiah Wilson and Thomas Fearn

YOUNG, JAMES and LUCY FEARN   April 13, 1791
        Surety, Francis Young

A LIST OF MARRIAGES SOLEMNIZED BY THE REV. WILLIAM HUBARD IN THE
PARISH OF NEWPORT IN THE COUNTY OF ISLE OF WIGHT, ETC., BEGINNING
FROM THE FIRST DAY OF JULY, 1785 TO THE FIRST DAY OF JULY, 1786.

1785

July	9	Davis Day and Julia Day
	21	John Smith and Julia Martin
	28	Edward Hannah and Mourning Matthews
August	2	James Copher and Mourning Pitman
	18	Lazarus Holloway and Sarah Brown
	18	John Wrench and Mary Pasteur
	25	John Parkinson and Catherine Whitley
	25	George Godby and Anne Edwards
September	3	John Oliver and Francis Lee
	29	Arthur Tomlin and Angelina Barmer
	29	John Daniel and Bathesheba Mintz
October	15	William Jordan and Martha Campbell
	18	Thomas English and Rebecca Boon
	22	Josiah Waile and Mary Driver
November	1	Frederick Hall and Peggy Jordan
	8	Benjamin Waller and Mary Womble
	16	Willis Coffield and Elizabeth Jordan
	24	William Goodwin and Frances Casey
December	3	L'Anson Edwards and Anne Pitman
	15	Arthur Crumpler and Mary Pursell
	18	Peter Woodward and Mary Turner
	20	Humphrey Revell and Eady Tomlin
	22	Elias Bowden and Celia Lawrence
	24	William Stallings and Mary Person
	25	John Dennis (?) and Jane Jackson
	25	Thomas Bounds and Elizabeth Avery

1786

January	3	Samuel Matthews and Peggy Parr
	3	William Binthall and Catherine Watkins
	5	Bracey Whitley and Rebecca Edwards
	5	Joseph Smith and Esther Hawkins
	7	Joseph Stringfield and Frances Dews

January	7	Jesse Atkinson and Sarah Applewhaite
	14	Joshua Hunt and Holland Holliday
	28	Benjamin Ward and Rebecca Edwards
	31	Joshua Gay and Amelia Bullock
February	27	John Bulger and Mary Bounds
March	2	Benjamin Cox and Rebecca Davis
	2	Nicholas Smith and Catherine Joyner
	21	Figuers Lewis and Patsey Driver
	23	Robert Lawrence and Sarah Eley
April	2	Nathaniel Pruden and Rhoda Bradley
	8	Thomas James and Mary Brantley
	11	Stephen Bell and Jemima Ingram
	27	Armstrong Edwards and Honour Turner
	29	Joseph Clark and Julia Coggin
May	11	Jesse Ewell and Mary Hodsden
	20	Michael Edwards and Betsey Jones
	21	William Carstopherine and Katherine Binn
June	1	James Wilson and Faithy Banks
	3	Thomas Campbell and Elizabeth Pitt
	8	Thomas Hicks and Mary Gwaltney
	10	William Bidgood and Elizabeth Jones
	15	Hugh Montgomery and Sally Gray
	28	John Newman and Keziah Bridger
July	4	Benjamin Harrison and Mary Eley
	8	William Atkinson and Nancy Lightfoot
	16	Mason Pinner and Catherine Powell
	18	Ishmiah Pitt and Mary Fulgham
	20	Thomas Nevill and Rhody Lawrence
	27	Thomas Godwin and Jennetilbua Jack-- (?)
August	5	Shadrack Harrison and Elizabeth Hobbs
	17	William Pinner and Tabitha Granberry
	19	Hezekiah Holladay and Mary Bagnall
	24	John Broadfield and Elizabeth Holladay
	29	John Gay and Rhody Bowden
	29	Thomas Lingo (Lupo) and Sarah Allmond
	31	Jeremiah Pinner and Elizabeth Pinner
September	2	Jacob Stringfield and Frances Bidgood
	7	William Bullock and Catherine Powell
	7	Robert Babb and Polly Hough
	21	John Gay and Joanna Goodson
	21	William Wilkinson and Rachel Parker
	28	Russell Godby and Nancy Stuckey
October	7	Sampson Harrison and Comfort Edwards
	7	John Clark and Peggy Norsworthy
	19	William Tankard and Marth Milner
	21	William Hill and Betsey Everett
	25	William Campbell and Catherine Pitt
	26	Edward Gay and Chloe Copher
	26	Edwin Godwin and Elizabeth Hunter
	29	Dolphin Driver and Jemima Whitfield
November	6	Samuel Haile and Elizabeth Matthews
	11	James Davis and Constance Barlow
	18	William Woodward and Martha Ward
	25	Henry Howard and Fanny Willet
	25	William Patterson and Frances Gibbs

November	26	Thomas Milner and Elizabeth Wilkinson
	30	John Vellines and Olive Thomas
	30	Thomas Brantley and Betsey Willet
December	6	Peter Cunningham and Louisa Fulgham
	14	Willis Parnall and Sarah Brown
	14	Mathew Thomas and Anne Gwaltney
	16	William Bagnall and Nelly Newman
	23	William James and Mary Hawkins
	26	Charles Bagnall and Amelia Godwin
	28	Samuel Everett and Betsey Shivers
	28	Thomas Davis and Mary Joyner
	30	James Clayton and Harly Goodrich

1787

January	4	William Slease (?) and Sally Holloway
	6	Thomas Garner and Mary Hall
	6	William Woodward and Tamer Cole
	7	Peter Shivers and Amelia Holliford
	11	Thomas Smith and Ann Edwards
	13	Thomas Flood and Elizabeth Gale
	18	Jesse Whitehead and Esther Marshall
	20	Peter Hobbs and Charlotte McCoy
February	6	Thomas Whitney Gale and Sarah Davis
	10	John Wootten and Elizabeth Jordan
March	3	Joel Newsum and Mary Eley
	5	Jesse Edwards and Mary Gwaltney
	6	Thomas Rider and Courtney Jones
April	3	John Francis Gabriels and Pamelia Smith
	7	Samuel Bidgood and Mary Carroll
	12	William Phillips and Mary Thompson
	14	John Wrenn and Patience Carroll
	20	James Cooks and Sarah Davis
	24	Joseph Brown and Catherine Parnall
	31	Simon Westray and Mary Saunders
June	2	Sampson Bones and Dolly Bowzer
	4	Solomon Wilson and Anne Riddick
	19	Anthony Holladay and Anne Godfrey
	30	Edmund Stuckley and Elizabeth Richards

A LIST OF MARRIAGES SOLEMNIZED BY THE SOCIETY OF PEOPLE CALLED QUAKERS, FROM THE 1ST OF JULY, 1785 TO THE 1ST OF JULY, 1786.

1786

February	26	Joseph Denson and Anne Pretlow
March	2	Lemuel Council and Julia Winbourne
	3	John Jordan and Elizabeth Trother
November	29	William Parter (Porter) and Mary Faulk

1787

November	28	Joseph Pretlow and Elizabeth Scott

MARRIAGES SOLEMNIZED BY THE REV. WILLIAM HUBARD FROM JULY, 1787
TO JULY, 1788.

1787

July	3	Josiah Cutchins and Ann Hall
	7	Nathaniel Jones and Priscilla Fones
	14	Rowland Reynolds and Martha Godwin
	17	David Williams and Prudence Harvey

| August | 11 | Henry Gray and Elizabeth Brown |

September	1	William Groce and Sarah Frizzell
	8	Luke Taylor and Bethiah Crocker
	17	Jeremiah Godwin and Ann Blow

October	20	George Pettitt and Nancy Partlow
	25	Lemuel Hart and Mary Pretlow
	25	John Armstrong and Unity Brantley
	27	Isaac Lowry and Jenny Abbington

| November | 17 | Thomas Gaskins and Milly Fulgham |
| | 20 | Richard Carter and Sarah Little |

December	1	Ishmaiah Pitt and Betsey Stoakley
	1	George Baines and Martha Reynolds
	6	Josiah Applewhaite and Polly Gibbs
	8	William Hatchell and Holland Lawrence
	11	Jesse Turner and Lucy Brown
	15	Stephen Smith and Betsey G. Godwin
	22	John Mallicote and Mary Gray
	25	Jesse Gray and Patsey Davis

1788

| January | 19 | Joseph Mainyard and Charlotte Norsworthy |
| | 29 | Horatio Green and Mary Howell |

February	19	Robert Nicholson and Mary Butler
	20	James Pyland and Sally White
	21	Vines Turner and Ann Adams

| March | 16 | Joseph Person and Polly Clark |

April	10	Rix Lawrence and Lilly Woodrop
	12	John Johnson and Ann Atkinson
	19	Norman McCloud and Patty Murry
	25	Thomas Boyd and Milly Hutchings

| August | 20 | Benjamin Tynes and Elizabeth Hill |

| September | 20 | Edmund Godwin and Holland Wills |

| October | 13 | Abel James and Cornelia Kepp |
| | 18 | Thomas Jacobs and Ann Mary Pitt |

November	6	Willis Corbell and Ann Jarvis
	15	John Stroud and Nancy Norseworthy
	20	Scarsbrook Jolliff and Sarah Tarlton

| December | 4 | Mallachi Fife and Mary Hawkins |

```
December      13  James Matthews and Ann Brantley
              17  Josiah Red and Priscilla English
              18  William Crocker and Elizabeth Wilson
              23  Samuel Bradley and Lucy Pitt
              25  Garrett J. Van Wagenum and Martha Todd
              28  William Talliferro and Elizabeth H. Cocke
```

1789

```
January       11  Benjamin Wootten and Mary Carter
              15  Peyton Randolph and Betsey Holland
              29  Samuel Blow and Mary Ridley Hart

February       8  John Chapman and Fanny Babb

March         12  John Cocks and Elizabeth Moreing

April         11  Isaac Johnson and Daphney Trusty
              19  Henry Lynn and Peggy Applewhaite

May            5  Jesse Toller and Elizabeth Garner
              31  Elias Saunders and Martha Watkins
```

MARRIAGES SOLEMNIZED BY WILLIS WILLS, METHODIST MINISTER.
Nansemond County:

```
1789  June 8         James Buxton and Jane Avery
1789  April -        William Coffield and Mary Lawrence
1790  September 12   Thomas Bullock and Peggy Evans
1791  February --    Thomas Colding (Cowling) and Charlotte Everett
1792  February 23    Jordan Parr and Lois Jordan
1795  October --     John Johnson and Mary Darby
```

Isle of Wight County:

1791

```
September    24  John Davis and Mary Uzzell
May          23  Benjamin Weston and Charlotte Godwin
July         26  Robert Pope and Elizabeth Giles
December      6  Thomas Hancock and Nancy Outland
September(?) 14  John Matthews and Mary Davis
March        30  Willis Holliford and Elizabeth Whitley
-----        23  Adam McCoy and Sarah Jolly
August        8  Jesse Murphrey and Louisa Cutchins
-----------      William Smith and Patsey Norsworthy
October      18  James Clayton and Elizabeth Uzzell
December     26  John Lawrence and Sarah Groce
```

1794

```
March        28  Thomas Bounds and Sarah Gale
June         13  John Parkinson and Caty Edwards
September     5  John Godwin and Polly Copeland
December     27  John Bullock and Mary Bridger
----         10  John Clark and Elizabeth Edwards
November     28  James Smith and Mary Chapman
```

1795

```
January       1  William Pinhorn and Keziah Edwards
----         --  William Matthews and Mary Pope
```

```
April       12  Thomas Gale and Patsey Gale
February    21  John Cook and Rachel Green
December    30  John H. Jemica and Anne Toller
```

Surry County:

1789

```
October      9  James Warren and Katy Andrews
```

MARRIAGE SOLEMNIZED BY BENJAMIN BARNES, METHODIST MINISTER.

```
1795 August 18      Robert Carr and Anne Holleman
```

MARRIAGES SOLEMNIZED BY NATHANIEL BERRYMAN, METHODIST MINISTER.

```
1795 June 25         William Maggett and Priscilla Hardy
---- ---- --         James Bennett and Anne Wright
179- September 26    Robert Heath and Rosey Dowty
```

MARRIAGES SOLEMNIZED BY PEOPLE CALLED QUAKERS.

```
1788 October 30      Samuel Nixon and Peggy Jordan
1789 April 25        Stephen Shepherd and Esther Winborne
1790 March 2         Thomas Peele and Lydia Johnson
1791 June 1          Lemuel Jones and Sally Denson
1791 October 10      Robert Jordan and Elizabeth Copeland
1792 ---- -          William Wrenn and Lydia Johnson
```

MARRIAGES SOLEMNIZED BY THE REV. WILLIAM HUBARD. JULY, 1789 TO
JULY 1790.

1789

```
August      15  Thomas Jordan and Celia Fulgham Casey

October     23  Frederick Jones and Holland Fulgham

November    10  Lazarus Levey and Keziah Harvey

December     3  Benjamin Brock and Martha Holleman
             5  James Johnston and Betsey Day
            17  James Carrell and Patsey Mangam
            22  Mathew Turner and Nancey Brown
            22  John Tomlin and Chloe Westray
            24  Skelton Edwards and Mary Shelly
            26  Robert Flake and Rebecca Dews
            26  Richard Brantley and Jemima Holladay
            31  William Cornwell and Mary Brown
```

1790

```
January      7  Michael Everett and Peggy Jordan Cowling
            12  Giles Daniel and Mary Jordan
            23  Copeland Whitfield and Pamelia Wills
            30  Joshua Duggin and Sally Jolliff
            30  John Davis and Ann Gray
            30  Lewis Chapman and Lucy Mangam
```

| February | 7 | William Crocker and Elizabeth Allen |
| | 23 | Michael Fulgham and Patsey Jordan |

1790

March	6	George Powell and Martha Batten
	27	James Akinson and Martha Applewhaite
	31	Richard Mathews and Elizabeth Parr
April	1	John Bullock and Elizabeth Johnson
May	6	James Delk and Martha Bell
June	24	Samuel Gray and Mary Mangam
July	22	Samuel Hampton and Patsey Powell
August	8	Thomas Mallicote and Milly Lupo
September	9	Thomas Gale and Chloe Fatherie
	20	William Harris and Mary Jordan
	23	Samuel Hampton and Eady Debirg--(?)
	23	John Riggon and Elizabeth Warren
	25	Joseph Godwin and Letitia Williams
October	17	James Holland and Polly Harris
November	11	Moody Copher and Martha Gwaltney
	20	David Jones and Fanny Barlow
December	16	William Clack (Clark) and Sally Gwaltney
	23	David Edwards and Chloe Chapman
	25	Josiah Davis and Polly Thomas
	28	William Dixon and Elizabeth Pope

1791

January	22	George Braswell and Conney Cofer
	25	James Hancock and Chace Womble
	27	Richard Rogers and Cherry Wrenn
	26	Thomas McClenchey and Nancy Bowden
	27	Joseph Driver and Priscilla Whitfield
February	6	John Lawrence and Polly Outland
	17	Hermon Hargrave and Diana Copher
	19	Thomas Munford and Nancy Shelly
	20	Copeland Whitfield and Catherine Howard
	24	John Peirce and Sally Johnson
March	26	John Hilton and Peggy Robertson
April	2	Jordan Thomas and Mary Hancock
	2	Peter Sampson and Angelina Atkinson
	3	Michael Kelly and Sally Braswell
	7	John Provan and Patsey Holladay Parr
	18	James Young and Lucy Fearn
	21	Benjamin Mathews and Tempy Nevill
March	14	Lemuel Bailey and Elizabeth Elliott
	25	Solomon Newman and Lydia Jones
	28	Thomas McWilliams and Jane Hubard
	30	David Bradley and Elizabeth Harrison

June	3	William Patrick and Margaret Easson
	30	John Turner and Mary Lawrence
July	5	Sampson Wilson and Winney Brantley
	23	James Askew and Polly Garnes
August	20	Nathaniel Wills and Mary Pedin
	25	Jesse Godwin and Mary Godwin of Nansemond Co.
	27	Jesse Atkinson and Mary Ward
September	24	Josiah Mangam and Elizabeth Abbet (?)
	28	William Bryant and Elizabeth Stuckey
	29	Phillip Thomas and Lucy Holleman
October	6	Jesse Clark and Judith Foster
	27	William Holloway and Sally Bennett
	27	Josiah Gray and Martha Everett
December	1	Mills Holladay and Martha Wrenn
	3	Jacob Dickinson and Mary Whitfield
	5	John Nelson and Mary Whitfield alias Miller
	10	John Gibbs and Polly Driver
	18	James Gray and Sally Goodwin Wills
	24	Thomas Casey and Celia Wallace
	28	John Holleman and Nancey Thomas
	29	James Morris and Sweeting Duke

1792

January	5	Skelton Delk and Angelina Gray
	7	Thomas Darden and Barsheba Wills
	14	George Lawrence and Sally Beal
	19	Mathew Wright and Sarah Baldwin
	19	Frederick Taylor and Frankey Womble
	24	Benjamin Barlow and Frankey Jones
	24	James Atkinson and Milly Mallicote
February	7	James Barlow and Mary Gibbs
	18	James Hodges and Jane Brown (Surry)
	18	Edmund Mason and Frances Young
	23	John Saunders and Holland Britt
March	10	Shelly White and Polly Brown
	22	Bennett Young and Polly Benn Godwin
	27	William Goodrich and Polly Duggin
April	5	Henry Edwards and Nancy Harrison
	12	John Farrow (?) and Tabitha Brown
	21	Dudley Whitaker and Polly Wills
May	12	Joseph Gray and Frances White
June	2	Joseph Miniard and Amelia Cutchins
July	5	William Lear Campbell and Mary Jordan
	26	William Mallory and Mary Bryan
	28	Robert Newton Cook and Elizabeth Norsworthy
August	9	Isaac Askew and Elizabeth Newman
	14	Thomas Graham and Sarah Barnes
	16	James Bell and Rebecca Lancaster
	30	James Reid and Fanny Wescott

October	20	Andrew Bryan and Elizabeth Champan (?)
	21	George Goodrich and Nancy Turner
	28	Machen Fearn and Ann Moreland
November	1	Jesse Cowling and Elizabeth George
	22	James Bidgood and Nancy Dews
December	4	Abraham Pruden and Unice Pruden
	6	Henry Coggan and Elizabeth Briggs
	8	William Godfrey and Patsey Newman
	18	Henry Bradley and Patience Pitt
	20	William Hardy and Sarah Dering
	22	James Garner and Sally Parnell
	24	Nicholas Goodson and Elizabeth Bullock
	24	Josiah Holladay and Martha Daniel
	27	Thomas Brantley and Mary Lupo
	29	Jeremiah Wombwell and Nancy Mountford

1793

January	24	John Hockaday and Mary Orr
	24	Daniel Herring and Hannah Hardy
	27	William Gaston (Garton?) and Mary Hodsden
February	7	John Applewhaite and Mary Godwin
	14	Lemuel Batten and Tatty Brown
	14	Drury Crocker and Lucy Barlow
	19	John Duck and Charity Darden
	21	John Sherrod and Temperance Shivers
	23	Mathew Fulgham and Rebecca Westray
	27	Wright Godwin and Polly Godwin
	28	Joseph Lawrence and Sally Sykes
March	9	Person Jones and Elizabeth Jones
	21	Thomas Best and Polly Shivers
April	17	Thomas Wilson and Sarah Hutchinson
	28	Seymore Powell and Sally Briggs
May	16	John Stevens and Mary Mountfort
	18	John Hancock and Nancy Williams
	25	Jonathan Wood and Martha Bococke
June	4	John Clark and Ann Godwin
	6	Henry Barnes and Fanny Channell
July	7	Benjamin Banks and Nancy Jones
	20	Thomas Wombwell and Nancy Outland
August	18	John Hutchinson and Peggy James
	21	James Harvey and Sally Godfrey
October	1	Joseph Godwin and Elizabeth Pitt
	7	Thaddeus Powell and Mary Powell
December	19	William Burnett and Frances Edwards
	24	Isham Jordan and Mary Shields
	26	Jacob Copher and Milly Braswell

1794

January	2	Elias Johnson and Caty Tomlin

January	4	William Gibbs and Lois Wills
	14	Benjamin Shelly and Elizabeth Gwaltney
	16	Rix Lawrence and Rachel Wilkinson

February   6   Freeman Gwaltney and Patty Brown

March   1   John Worrell and Patsey Griffin

April	12	William Carstaphen and Anne Archer
	17	Jesse Edwards and Polly Copher
	19	Lewis (?) Jordan and Frances Atkinson

| June | 1 | Samuel Batten and Mary Powell |
| | 5 | Phillip Moody and Polly Gwaltney |

July	6	William Jones and Elizabeth Michael
	10	John Outland and Sally Babb
	17	Wilson Murry and Priscilla Hawkins
	27	James Pitt and Mary Michael

August   9   James Williams and Mildred Taylor

September 25   Randolph Fitchett and Rebecca Bell

November	8	William Pinner and Catherine Bradley
	13	Richard Thomas and Chloe Stringfield
	13	John Farrow and Nancy Beal
	20	William Carter and Elizabeth Smith
	22	George Benn and Mary Ann Bashfoot (?)
	27	Mesheck Goodrich and Sally Shelly

| December | 11 | James Powell and Suckey Betts |
| | 25 | James Jenkins and Sally Coggan |

1795

January   15   Jesse Thomas and Elizabeth Presson

February	12	John Woodward and Esther King
	22	Lemuel Clark and Mary Williams
	26	William Stallings and Mary Davidson

March	7	Gustavus Adolphus Brown and Abby Tucker
	7	William Morris and Ann Wilson
	9	Isaac Jones and Elizabeth Thomas
	23	Lazarus Levy and Sarah Drummond
	24	Solomon Bracey and Lydia Turner

April   30   Josiah Cowling and Christianna Mackie

| June | 6 | Davis Jones and Clary Banks |
| | 27 | George Edwards and Elizabeth Smith |

MARRIAGES SOLEMNIZED BY WILLIS WILLS, A METHODIST MINISTER.

1787 August 10   Ishmael Moody and Sarah Brantley

1788 December 24   John Pinhorn and Mary Uzzell

| 1789 | October 11 | Joel Phillips and Amelia Nevill |
| | May 28 | George Whitley and Elizabeth Davis |

93

1790	March 10	Charles Murphrey and Polly Moody
	March 20	Isaac Vellines and Sarah Moody
	July 8	William Whitley and Sarah Turner
	August 10	Charles Groce and Sarah Smelly
	October 8	Thomas Carrell and Silvia Uzzell
	October 9	Nathaniel Gray and Lydia Driver
	October 23	Dempsey Murphrey and Rachel Nelms
1791	January 29	Addison Dowty and Elizabeth Pitman
	March 30	Nicholas Smith and Martha House
	August 5	John Saunders Whitley and Barsheba Bateman
	September 1	William Bagnall and Mildred Dowty
	November 24	John Johnson and Ann Bidgood
	February 3	James Allmand and ---- Morrison
	September 24	John Davis and Mary Davis
1792	February 21	Thomas Flint and Elizabeth Godwin
	February 19	Isham Copeland and Charlotte Fulgham
	February 14	John Reynolds and Elizabeth Whitley
	February 18	Samuel Smith and Constant Davis
	September 15	Murphry Dickson and Lydia Haile
	January 14	Thomas Davis and Charlotte Womble
	March 24	Miles Milner and Lucy Phillips
1790	December 21	Henry Thompson and Louisa Giles

A MARRIAGE SOLEMNIZED BY JOHN McCABE.

| 1792 | January 5 | Richard Cason and Elizabeth Holland |

MARRIAGES SOLEMNIZED BY NATHANIEL BERRYMAN. M. M.

1795	October 22	William Seaward and Cherry Pitman
	December 27	Richard Pierce and Polly Wrenn
1796	February 5	Aaron Moore and Patsey Tucker
1795	December 13	Thomas Stott and Polly Pitman
1796	February 6	J'Anson Edwards and Sarah Hardy
	May 7	Richard Parr and Polly Heath
	July 7	William Taylor and Martha Lancaster
	August 13	Allen Davis and Peggy Lane
	November 1	William Parr and Florentina Callcote
	November 25	Henry Turner and Polly Kimball
	December 17	John Kimball and Jenny Smith
	December 31	Nathaniel Jones and Polly Davis

MARRIAGES SOLEMNIZED BY CHARLES MURPHREY.

1796	December 10	Thomas Elsberry and Martha Powell
	December 31	Henry Jemmicka and Keziah Garner
1797	February 11	Seth Hunter and Elizabeth Powell
	February 3	William West and Fanny Parnell
	February 13	Britain Britt and Jenny Edmunds
	April 6	Robert Jordan and Peggy Jordan
	June 17	John Clark and Betsey Hudson
	August 11	John Babb and Betsey Pope
	August 15	Lewis Harris and Mary Hatchell
	December 9	John Anthony and Sally Hunter

MARRIAGES SOLEMNIZED BY DAVID BRADLEY.

1797	January 5	Thomas Jones and Elizabeth Chapman
	March 7	Cary Barlow and Elizabeth Davis
	March 9	Micajah Mountfort and Sally Mahone
	June 15	John Goodson and Elizabeth Randolph Bell
	November 9	Andrew Woodley and Elizabeth Hill Harrison
1798	January 4	Samuel Smith and Nancy Bond (widow)

MARRIAGE RETURNS BY WILLIAM BLUNT.   (Year not given.)

	January 31	Thomas Joiner and Peggy Morrison
	April 8	Sellaway Bracey and Nancy Moody
1798	March 27	John Weeks and Nancy Moody

MARRIAGES SOLEMNIZED BY NATHANIEL BERRYMAN, M. M.

| 1797 | February 23 | William Mahone and Wilmuth Womble |
| 1798 | April 28 | Thomas Shelly and Frances Edwards |

A MARRIAGE SOLEMNIZED BY JAMES HUNTER.

| 1794 | September 15 | James Godwin and Elizabeth Godwin |

LIST RETURNED BY WILLIS WILLS.

1795	August 12	Elisha Godwin and Elizabeth Stokeley
	June 18	Charles Bryant and Charlotte Stuckie
	November 9	Randolph Reynolds and Martha Dickinson
	September 19	Samuel Weston and Rhoda Bains
	December 26	William Allmand and Elizabeth Toler
1796	January 12	Joseph Elsberry and --- Everett of Nansemond
	February --	John Pierce and Mildred Joiner
	March 31	Richard Corbell and Adar Stokely
	May --	Thomas Pinner and Elizabeth Bullock of Nansemond Co.
	May 6	Thomas Hall and ---- Goodson
	June 26	Purnell Pitt and Sarah Butler
	August 29	Barden Bullock and Betsey Pinner
	December 10	James Martin and Polly Beagnall (?)
1797	October 28	Edwin Godwin and Nancy Stokeley
1798	March 1	James Gray and Esther Pitt
	July 14	Willis Godwin and Sally Daniel
	October 3	George Darby and Julia Williams
	November 17	John Reynolds and Polly Jordan
1799	February 12	Charles Rountree and Elizabeth Flint
	March 7	John Morrison and E---- Campbell

MARRIAGES SOLEMNIZED BY ISAAC VELLINES.

1798	July 8	Daniel Sumner and Rebecca Tomlin
1799	January 24	Elias Daniel and Polly Holland
	March 2	John Boykin Eley and Patsey Fletcher
	March 30	Charles Fulgham and Caty Powell

95

MARRIAGES SOLEMNIZED BY NATHANIEL BERRIMAN, M. M.

1799 September 10   Joseph Copher and Jerusha Lancaster
      December 26'   Thomas Harding and Nancy Taylor
      December 28   George Gray and Patsey Carrell

1800 April 7   Henry Jones and Sally Davis

MARRIAGES SOLEMNIZED BY WILLIAM BLUNT.

1799 September 12   Lemuel Womble and Flora Parr

1800 January 2   Michael Rogers and Polly Clark

MARRIAGES SOLEMNIZED BY WILLIAM POWELL (Year not given.)

      May 13   Willis Groce and Sally Jordan
      November 28   Samuel Stamp and Patsey Hutchings
      December 24   Jordan Parr and Mary Johnson

1800 May 20   Samuel Smith and Holland Davis

A MARRIAGE SOLEMNIZED BY CHARLES MURPHREY

1800 December 18   Benjamin Norsworthy and Frances Allmand

A MARRIAGE SOLEMNIZED BY ISAAC VELLINES

1800 October 10   James Bennett and Fereby Deford

MARRIAGES SOLEMNIZED BY WILLIS WILLS

1799 July 2   Samuel McCoy and Ann Godwin
      July 3   John Briggs and Elizabeth Heath
      August 17   Arthur Benn and Patsey Tate (?)

1800 January 15   Joseph Norsworthy and Lydia Chapman
      April 30   Jonathan Godwin and Patsey Holladay
      August 10   William Goodwin and Patsey Bunkley
      August 12   William Addison and Nancy Gray
      October --   Randolph Reynolds and Rhoda Baines
      October 28   Randall Reynolds and Rhoda Weston

QUAKER RECORDS

Minute Book - Lower Virginia Meeting
1673-1709

BELSON, EDMOND, son of Elizabeth Belson of Nansemond County and
MARY CREW, the daughter of Mary Tooke of Isle of
Wight County.
13 day of 10 mo. 1684   p. 64

BELSON, EDMOND of Nansemond County and JEAN RIDDICK, daughter of
Robert Riddick of Nansemond County.
11 day of 5 mo. 1689   p. 133

BOGUE, WILLIAM of North Carolina and SARAH DUKE, daughter of
Thomas Duke of Nansemond County.
15 day of 12 mo. 1727/8   p. 158

BRAISE (BRASSEUR), FRANCIS, son of Hugh Braise of Isle of Wight
and ELIZABETH WIGGS, daughter of Henry Wiggs.
15 day of 7 mo. 1713   p. 150

BRESSIE, HUGH, nephew of William Bressie and SARAH CAMPION of
Isle of Wight.
14 day of 3 mo. 1680   p. 89

BUFKIN, LEAVEN and DOROTHY NEWBY, daughter of William Newby of
Nansemond County.
17 day of 2 mo. 1688   p. 81

CHAPMAN, BENJAMIN and MARY COPELAND. Letter proving marriage
dated 12 day of 3 mo. 1703.
                                         p. 159

COLLINS, JOHN, whose father-in-law was JOHN BARNES and MARY
TOOKE of Surry County.
14 day of 12 mo. 1682   p. 116

DENSON, JAMES, son of Frances Denson, widow of Isle of Wight
County and SARAH DRYTON.
15 day of 11 mo. 1707   p. 148

DENSON, JOHN, son of Frances Denson, widow of Isle of Wight
County and MARY BRYDLE, daughter of Francis Brydle
of Isle of Wight County.
12 day of 9 mo. 1692   p. 130

DENSON, WILLIAM, son of John Denson of Isle of Wight County and
AMEY SMALL, daughter of Benjamin Small of Nansemond
County.
20 day of 12 mo. 1723   p. 152

GAY, THOMAS, son of Joane Lawrence of Isle of Wight County and
    REBECCA PAGE, daughter of Thomas Page of Isle of
    Wight County.
    11 day of 11 mo. 1699   p. 136

HARRIS, JOHN and ELIZABETH CHURCH of Isle of Wight County.
    13 day of 4 mo. 1689   p. 125

HALL, MOSES - I have given my consent to Moses Hall as concerning
    marriage with my daughter MARGARET DUKE.
    7 day of 11 mo. 1707   Signed, Thomas Duke, Sr.

HOLLOWELL, HENRY, son of Thomas Hollowell of Elizabeth River and
    ELIZABETH CUTCHINS, daughter of Thomas Cutchins of
    Chuckatuck, Nansemond County.
    7 day of 8 mo. 1680   p. 90

HOLLOWELL, HENRY of Elizabeth River and ELIZABETH SCOTT of
    Nansemond County.
    20 day of 2 mo. 1693   p. 125

JONES, ROBERT and MARTHA RICE of Nansemond County
    10 day of 5 mo. 1683   p. 117

JORDAN, JAMES, son of Thomas Jordan of Chuckatuck and ELIZABETH
    RATCLIFF of Isle of Wight County.
    29 day of 3 mo. 1688   p. 69

JORDAN, JAMES and ANN ROSETER of Nansemond County.
    14 day of 7 mo. 1701

JORDAN, JOHN, son of Thomas Jordan and MARGARET BURGH, both of
    Chuckatuck.
    9 day of 12 mo. 1688   p. 66

JORDAN, JOSEPH, son of Joseph Jordan of North Carolina and MARY
    RIX, daughter of Abraham Rix of Isle of Wight County.
    10 day of 2 mo. 1723   p. 155

JORDAN, MATHEW, son of Thomas Jordan of Chuckatuck and DOROTHY
    BUFKIN, widow of Nansemond County.
    6 day of 7 mo. 1699   p. 135

JORDAN, MATHEW of Nansemond County and SUSANNA BRESSY of Isle of
    Wight County, a widow.
    17 day of 3 mo. 1702   p. 139

JORDAN, RICHARD, son of Thomas Jordan of Chuckatuck and REBECCA
    RATCLIFF, daughter of Richard Ratcliff of Isle of
    Wight County.
    22 day of 6 mo. 1706   p. 146

JORDAN, ROBERT, son of Thomas Jordan of Chuckatuck and CHRISTIAN
    OUDELANT, daughter of Thomas Taberer of Isle of Wight.
    9 day of 12 mo. 1687   p. 67

JORDAN, ROBERT, son of Thomas Jordan of Chuckatuck and MARY
    BELSON, daughter of Edmond Belson, decd.
    10 day of 5 mo. 1690   p. 128

JORDAN, THOMAS SR. married MARGARET, daughter of Robert Brashier
    of Nansemond County.   abt. 1658   p. 62 &
                                                         81
JORDAN, THOMAS, son of Thomas of Chuckatuck and ELIZABETH BURGH,
    daughter of William Burgh.
    6 day of 10 mo. 1679   p. 87

KENERLY, JOSEPH of Dorchester County, Province of Maryland, and
        SARAH RATCLIFF, daughter of Richard Ratcliff of Isle
        of Wight County.
        20 day of 7 mo. 1696   p. 132

MAREDITH, JOSEPH, son of Samson Meredith of Nansemond County,
        and SARAH DENSON, daughter of Francis Denson of Isle
        of Wight County.
        11 day of 4 mo. 1696   p. 131

MURRELL, GEORGE, son of George Murrell of Surry County, and
        MARY WATERS, daughter of Walter Waters of Isle of
        Wight County.
        16 day of 2 mo. 1704   p. 141

MURRY, JOHN and ELIZABETH GARRETT, daughter of William Garrett
        of Isle of Wight County.
        22 day of 6 mo. 1678
        (This name is written Yarrett in Isle of Wight
        records.)   p. 85

MURRY, JOHN and ELIZABETH HITCHENS of Isle of Wight County.
        15 day of 2 mo. 1686   p. 77

NEWBY, NATHAN, son of William Newby of Nansemond County and
        ELIZABETH HOLLOWELL, daughter of Alice Hollowell of
        Elizabeth River.
        13 day of 10 mo. 1678   p. 127

NEWMAN, THOMAS and MARY RATCLIFF of Isle of Wight County.
        13 day of 2 mo. 1699   p. 134

OUTLAND, CORNELIUS and HANNAH COPELAND.
        5 day of 3 mo. 1675   p. 80

OUTLAND, WILLIAM of Chuckatuck and CHRISTIAN TABERER, daughter of
        Thomas Taberer of Isle of Wight County.
        15 day of 9 mo. 1678   p. 86

PAGE, JOHN of Isle of Wight County and FFELECIA HALL, daughter
        of Moses Hall, decd. of Nansemond County.
        (No date given.)   p. 154

PAGE, THOMAS, son of Thomas Page of Isle of Wight County and
        ISABEL LAWRENCE, daughter of Henry Lawrence of Nanse-
        mond.
        15 day of 1 mo. 1702   p. 139

PERSON, JOHN, son of John Person of Isle of Wight County and
        MARY PARTRIDGE, daughter of Thomas Partridge of Surry
        County.
        10 day of 1 mo. 1692   p. 129

POPE, WILLIAM and MARY HAILE, both of Nansemond County.
        11 day of 2 mo. 1708   p. 147

POWELL, WILLIAM, son of Elizabeth Powell, widow and MARY PAGE,
        daughter of Thomas Page, both of Isle of Wight County.
        14 day of 2 mo. 1700   p. 137

RATCLIFFE, CORNELIUS of Isle of Wight and ELIZABETH JORDAN, widow.
        23 day of 9 mo. 1721   p. 151

RATCLIFFE, RICHARD, son of Richard Ratcliff of Terrascoe Neck
        and ELIZABETH HOLLOWELL, daughter of Henry Hollowell

of Isle of Wight County.
18 day of 7 mo. 1700   p. 138

RICKESIS, ABRAHAM, son of Isaac Rickesis and MARY BELSON, daughter
    of Edmond Belson, both of Nansemond County.
    16 day of 3 mo. 1703   p. 140

RICKESIS, JACOB, son of Isaac Rickesis and MARY EXUM, daughter
    of Jeremiah Exum of Isle of Wight County.
    14 day of 10 mo. 1699   p. 136

SANDERS, WILLIAM and MARY HALL of Nansemond County.
    9 day of 4 mo. 1682   p. 91

SIKES, THOMAS - Thomas Page testifies he was a subscriber on
    his certificate of marriage.
    9 day of 10 mo. 1705   p. 159

SMALL, BENJAMIN and ELIZABETH HOLLOWELL of Nansemond County.
    12 day of 1 mo. 1699   p. 131

SMALL, JOHN, son of John Small of Nansemond County and ALICE
    HOLLOWELL, daughter of Alice Hollowell of Elizabeth
    River.
    25 day of 12 mo. 1688   p. 126

SMALL, JOSEPH, son of John Small and ANN OWEN, daughter of
    Gilbert Owen of Nansemond Couty.
    18 day of 8 mo. 1722   p. 157

SCOTT, JOHN, son of William Scott of Chuckatuck and ELIZABETH
    BELSON, sister of Edmond Belson.
    19 day of 8 mo. 1682   p. 64

SCOTT, JOHN, son of William of Isle of Wight County and JOAN
    TOOK, daughter of Thomas Took.
    before 28 day of 4 mo. 1706   p. 44

SCOTT, WILLIAM, son of John Scott, decd., of Nansemond County
    and CHRISTIAN JORDAN, daughter of Robert Jordan.
    28 day of 6 mo. 1707   p. 147

TABERER, THOMAS of Isle of Wight County and MARGARET WOOD,
    widow of John Wood, after 1656.   p. 73

WHITE, THOMAS, son of John White of Isle of Wight County and
    RACHEL JORDAN, daughter of Joshua Jordan.
    13 day of 7 mo. 1719   p. 153

WIGGS, HENRY and CATHERINE GARRETT.
    3 day of 12 mo. 1674   p. 80

WILKINSON, WILLIAM, son of Henry Wilkinson, decd., of Nansemond
    County, and REBECCA POWELL, daughter of William
    Powell, of Isle of Wight County.
    21 day of 9 mo. 1723   p. 156

WOODSON, JOSEPH - Daniel Sanborne writes his consent for marriage
    of Joseph Woodson to his daughter MARY.
    9 day of 11 mo. 1706

(Date of marriage not given. Date on which
"liberty given to marry when they see fit.")

BALEY (BAILEY), TYRAL and PATIENCE BRASSEY.
15 day of 3 mo. 1746   p. 13

BRACEY, FRANCIS and ANN JORDAN.
------------------1743   p. 9

CHEADLES, JOHN and ELIZABETH HARGRAVE.
15 day of 1 mo. 1750   p. 18

CLAREY, BARNES and MARY JORDAN.
16 day of 5 mo. 1747   p. 15

COPELAND, JAMES and MARTHA JOHNSON.
17 day of 11 mo. 1744/5   p. 17

COPELAND, THOMAS and MARY MURREY.
18 day of 11 mo. 1749   p. 17

DENSON, BENJAMIN and MARY WHITEHEAD.
15 day of 8 mo. 1747   p. 15

DENSON, JOSEPH and CHRISTIAN ELEY.
19 day of 2 mo. 1744   p. 10

DENSON, WILLIAM and ANN WATKINS.
16 day of 5 mo. 1747   p. 15

DRAPER, THOMAS and PATIENCE DENSON.
6 day of 7 mo. 1739   p. 4

HARGRAVE, JESSE and NAOMEY SEBRELL.
16 day of 1 mo. 1748/9   p. 17

HARGRAVE, SAMUEL and SARAH PRETLOW.
5 day of 9 mo. 1741   p. 7

HOLLOWELL, ABSALOM and MARY HARGRAVE.
19 day of 2 mo. 1750   p. 18

HOLLOWELL, DENSON and MARTHA COFIELD.
16 day of 4 mo. 1752 (Intention of marriage
published for first time.)

HOLLOWELL, JOSEPH and MARTHA WILLIAMS.
2 day of 8 mo. 1740   p. 5

HOLLOWELL, WILLIAM and SARAH COFIELD.
16 day of 3 mo. 1751   p. 20

JOHNSON, JACOB and MARY DENSON.
3 day of 7 mo. 1741   p. 7

JOHNSON, LAZARUS and MARY OUTLAND.
15 day of 8 mo. 1747   p. 15

JOHNSON, ROBERT and CHRISTIAN OUTLAND.
17 day of 11 mo. 1744/5   p. 11

JORDAN, JOSIAH and MOURNING RICKS.
17 day of 2 mo. 1746   p. 13

JORDAN, MATHEW and MARY BRACY.
20 day of 9 mo. 1746   p. 14

JORDAN, PLEASANTS and MARY CORBIN.
3 day of 3 mo. 1739   p. 3

LADD, JESSE and MARGARET WHITFIELD.
20 day of 12 mo. 1752   p. 21

LAWRENCE, JOHN and MARTHA RICKS.
--- 10 mo. 1740   p. 5

MATTHIS, RICHARD and REBECCA PINNER.
4 day of 8 mo. 1739   p. 4

NEWBY, JOSEPH and PATIENCE JORDAN.
15 day of 12 mo. 1749   p. 18

NEWBY, THOMAS and MARY PRETLOW.
3 day of 9 mo. 1743   p. 9

OUTLAND, JOHN and ELIZABETH WILKINSON.
7 day of 3 mo. 1741   p. 6

OUTLAND, JOHN and ELIZABETH BRACEY.
21 day of 11 mo. 1747   p. 16

OUTLAND, THOMAS and ELIZABETH WHITE.
17 day of 11 mo. 1744/5   p. 11

OUTLAND, WILLIAM and MARY RATCLIFF.
5 day of 8 mo. 1738   p. 2

OUTLAND, WILLIAM and RACHEL WHITE.
4 day of 12 mo. 1741   p. 7

PINNER, JOHN and SARAH SCOTT.
-- 10 mo. 1740   p. 6

PLEASANTS, JOHN and ELIZABETH SCOTT.
-- 10 mo. 1740   p. 6

POPE, RICHARD and ANN WILLIAMS.   p. 14
16 day of 8 mo. 1746 (Intention of marriage
published for first time.)

PORTER, JOHN and BETTY DENSON.
1 day of 10 mo. 1743   p. 10

POWELL, JACOB and SARAH BULLOCK.
3 day of 3 mo. 1739   p. 3

PRETLOW, JOSEPH and SARAH SCOTT.
2 day of 9 mo. 1738   p. 2

PRETLOW, THOMAS and MARY RICKS.
17 day of 11 mo. 1744/5   p. 11

RICKS, RICHARD and ANN GARRETT.
19 day of 6 mo. 1751   p. 20

102

SCOTT, JAMES TOOK and CHRISTIAN NORSWORTHY.
4 day of 11 mo. 1738   p. 2

SCOTT, WILLIAM and ELIZABETH RICKS.
2 day of 10 mo. 1742   p. 8

SEBRELL, DANIEL and MARGARET JORDAN.
16 day of 2 mo. 1747   p. 14

SEBRELL, MOSES and SARAH HARGRAVE.
16 day of 3 mo. 1751   p. 20

WHITE, JOSHUA and MARY CORNWELL.
15 day of 1 mo. 1750   p. 18

WHITEHEAD, LEWIS and MARY WATKINS.
20 day of 1 mo. 1746   p. 12

WIGGS, WILLIAM and LIDIA SEBRELL.
5 day of 6 mo. 1742   p. 8

MINUTE BOOK - BURLEIGH, PRINCE GEORGE COUNTY

BAILEY, EDMOND of Southampton County and ELIZABETH WOMBLE.
19 day of 9 mo. 1762   p. 108

CLARY, JAMES of Southampton County and MARTHA, daughter of Peter
Stevenson.
21 day of 7 mo. 1760   p. 107

DAVIS, DAVID of Southampton County and LYDIA KITCHEN.
19 day of 12 mo. 1756   p. 99

HARRIS, MATHEW of Isle of Wight County and MARY HOUSE of Southampton
County.
22 day of 2 mo. 1755   p. 120

MINUTE BOOK - HENRICO MONTHLY MEETING

JORDAN, BENJAMIN, son of Benjamin Jordan of Isle of Wight County
and LYDIA PLEASANTS, daughter of Thomas Pleasants of
Henrico County.
6 day of 10 mo. 1741   p. 201

FROM
SOUTHAMPTON COUNTY MARRIAGE BONDS

BASS, THOMAS and SARAH ENGLISH, both of Isle of Wight County.
March 27, 1788.

CARR, THOMAS of Isle of Wight County and CHARLOTTE BEAL.
June 25, 1789.

CHAPMAN, JOHN and MARY SIMMONS, both of Isle of Wight County.
February 17, 1789.

COGGAN, WILLIAM and NANCY PIERCE, both of Isle of Wight County.
January 12, 1789.

COUNCIL, JOHN of Isle of Wight County and SALLY JOYNER.
January 29, 1784.

DANIELS, JOSHUA and SALLY FULGHAM, both of Isle of Wight County.
February 26, 1789.

DAVIS, DAVID and PRISCILLA GRAY of Isle of Wight County.
August 15, 1789.

ELEY, WILLIAM of Isle of Wight County and LUCY BRANCH.
April 1, 1778.

ENGLISH, JOHN and PRISCILLA COFFIELD, both of Isle of Wight County.
September 27, 1787.

GORDON, WILLIAM of Isle of Wight County and MARY PARSONS of Surry County.
April 22, 1788.

GWALTNEY, JAMES of Isle of Wight County and MARY WHITE.
January 15, 1789.

HOLLAND, EVERETT of Isle of Wight County and DARKEY BARRETT.
July 16, 1778.

HOLLEMAN, CHRISTOPHER of Isle of Wight County and ELIZABETH INMAN of Surry County.
October 21, 1787.

LAWRENCE, HARDY of Isle of Wight County and AMEY LOYD.
July 1, 1762.

NELMS, EZEKIEL of Nansemond County and ELIZABETH BRITT of Isle of Wight County.
July 27, 1788.

OUTLAND, WILLIAM and REBECCA STRINGFIELD, both of Isle of Wight County.
December 20, 1788.

TURNER, PIERCE and BETTY POWELL, both of Isle of Wight County.
September 11, 1787.

INDEX

-A-

Abbet (?), Elizabeth 91
Abbington, (Mrs.) 11
  Jane 73
  Jane Abigail 53
  Jenny 87
  Thomas 11
Abbitt, Elizabeth 73
Abel, James Jr. 71
Abraham, John 1
Adams, Ann 87
  John 1
  Thomas 1
Addison, William 57, 80,
  96
Akinson, James 90
Al----, Sally 66
Allen, Ann 13, 14
  Arthur 51
  Edward 53
  Elizabeth 6, 13, 63,
  90
  Henry 1, 8, 13
  Joan 51
  John 1
  Joseph 6, 14, 45
  Judith 45
  (Mrs.) Mary 8
  Thomas 1, 13
  William 74
Alley, Thomas 1
Allmand (see also Allmond)
  Aaron 1
  Ann 46
  Frances 96
  Isaac 1, 46
  James 39, 94
  Sophia 39
  William 95
Allmond (see also Allmand)
  James 57
  Sarah 85
  William 57, 66
Almand (see Allmand)
Altman, (Mrs.) 50
  John 50
Amis, Frances 41
  James 41
Andrews, Katy 89
Anthony, John 94
Applewhaite, Amy 14
  Ann 19, 35, 48, 51
  (Mrs.) Ann 30

Applewhaite (cont.)
  Arthur 1, 48, 53, 57,
  82
  Henry 1, 14, 19, 40
  Henry Jr. 5
  Holland 11
  John 49, 57, 92
  Josiah 57, 68, 87
  Martha 57, 90
  (Mrs.) Martha 35
  Mary 4, 41, 51, 53,
  79
  (Mrs.) Mary 5
  Mills 1
  Peggy 88
  Pheriba 49
  Priscilla 40
  Sally 24, 70
  Sarah 30, 85
  Thomas 1, 4, 11, 41
Appleyard, William 2
Archer, Anne 93
  Edward 1
  Mary 1
Armour, (Mrs.) Mary 27
  William 27
Armstrong, John 57, 87
Arrington, Elizabeth 12
  William 2, 12
Ashley,_____ 42
  Christopher 42
Askew, Aaron 57
  Isaac 91
  James 91
  John 2
  Jonas 57, 66
  Mary 77
  Mills 57
  Nicholas 2
  William 53
Atkins, Angelina 78
  Ann 71
  Christopher 2
  David 2
  John 61
  Joseph 63
Atkinson, Angelina 90
  Ann 31, 87
  Benjamin 31
  Frances 93
  Hannah 11
  James 2, 25, 57, 70, 91

Atkinson (cont)
  James Jr. 2
  Jesse 2, 57, 85, 91
  John 2, 11, 57
  Joseph 36
  Martha 22
  Mary 26, 36
  Samuel 26
  Sarah 25
  Siomon 2
  William 22, 85
Avery, Elizabeth 84
  Jane 88
Ayres, Frances 2, 9
  (Mrs.) Jane 9

-B-

B-----, Joseph 71
Babb, Ann 58
  Chloe 66
  Fanny 88
  John 94
  (Mrs.) Mary 19
  Nancy 75
  Robert 85
  Sally 93
  Sarah 19, 35
  William 35, 57
Bacon, Nathaniel Sr. 2
Bagnall, Charles 86
  Charlotte 74
  Easter 34
  James 2
  Juliana 37
  Mary 37, 85
  Nathan 2, 34, 37
  Polly 73
  Richard 37
  William 57, 67, 86, 94
Bailey, Barneby 2
  Benjamin 2
  Edmond 103
  John 2
  Lemuel 58, 90
  Tyral 101
  William 73, 75
  William Jr. 64, 76, 79,
  81

Bain (see Bains/Baines)
Bains/Baines, George 58, 87
  Henry 58, 63
  Rhoda 81, 95, 96
Baker, Ann 34
  Blake 3
  Catherine 23
  Charles 3
  Joseph 58
  Lawrence 23, 34
  Richard 3
Balding (see Borland)
Baldwin, Sarah 83, 91
  Silvia 57
  William 3, 57, 58, 66
Baley (see Bailey)
Ballard, Andrew 58
  Elisha 3
Banks, Benjamin 58, 92
  Clara 72
  Clary 93
  Faithy 85
  Nathaniel 58
Barcroft, Josiah 3
Barden, John 47
  Susanna 47
Barecroft, Charles 33, 41
  Elizabeth 41
  Jane 33
Barham, Thomas 3
Barkley, John 16
  Milly 16
Barlow, Ann 48
  Benjamin 58, 91
  Caty 95
  Constance 85
  (Mrs.) Elizabeth 3
  Fanny 90
  George 3, 63
  James 58, 60, 67, 76, 91
  John 58
  Lucy 58, 63, 92
  Martha 55
  Nancy 76
  Sampson 55, 58, 75
  Thomas 3, 58
  William 3, 48, 80
Barmer, Angelina 84
  Sarah 68
Barnes, Benjamin 89
  (Mrs.) Dian 9
  Henry 92
  John 3, 97
  Sarah 91
  Thomas 3
Barraud, Phillip 3, 58
Barrett, Darkey 104
Bashfoot(?), Mary Ann 93
Bass, Thomas 58, 103
Bateman, Barsheba 82, 94
  John 82
Batt, William 3
Batten,_____ 43
  Daniel 43, 48
  Lemuel 92
  Martha 77, 90
  Samuel 93
  Sarah 48
Battle, John 3
Baynton, Peter 3
Beagnall(?), Polly 95
Beal (see also Beale)
  Absalom 47
  Barnaby 67
  Benjamin 35, 57

Beal (cont.)
  Charlotte 103
  Elias 58
  Honour 47, 65
  James 69, 73
  Mary 35
  Nancy 93
  Priscilla 58
  Robert 65
  Sally 73, 91
Beale (see also Beal)
  Benjamin 3, 15, 31
  Benjamin Jr. 3
  John 3
  Mary 31
  Rachel 15
Beatman, John 59
Bechinoe, Edward 20
  George 21
  (Mrs.) Mary 20, 21
Beckett, Charles 3
Bell,_____ 4
  Alice 32
  Ann 12
  Benjamin 3, 12
  Elizabeth Randolph 95
  James 91
  John 4, 32
  Martha 90
  (Mrs.) Mary 6
  Micajah 59
  Rebecca 93
  Stephen 85
  William 3
Belson, Edmond 97, 98, 100
  Elizabeth 97, 100
  Mary 98, 100
Benn, Arthur 40, 96
  (Mrs.) Frances 40
  George 62, 83, 93
  James 3, 4
  (Capt.) James 52
  (Mrs.) Mary 52
Bennett,_____ 25
  (Mrs.) Alice 25
  Ambrose 4
  Edward 24
  James 59, 89, 96
  Jane 10
  John 15, 44, 53
  Lucy 44
  Martha 15
  Moses 4
  Richard 10
  Sally 91
  Silvestra 24
  William 59
Berkley (see Bunkley)
Berriman (see Berryman)
Berryman, Nathaniel 89, 94, 95, 96
  Robert 4
Best, Henry 4
  John 4
  Susanna 67
  Thomas 59, 92
Bethesea, (Mrs.) 47
  Robert 47
Betts, Suckey 93
Bevan, Hardy 4
  (Mrs.) Mary 21
  Peter 4
  Robert 4
  Thomas 21
Bidgood, Ann 71, 94
  Benjamin 59
  Frances 85

Bidgood (cont.)
  James 59, 92
  John Jr. 4
  Josiah 64
  Martha 72
  Micajah 72
  Samuel 59, 86
  William 4, 85
  William Sr. 4
Binn, Katherine 85
Binthall, William 84
Bird, Bethiah 49
  (Mrs.) Elizabeth 49, 51
  Jane 51
  Robert 28
  Susannah 28
Bland, Simon 82
  Thomas 59
Blow, Ann 87
  (Mrs.) Ann 46
  Elizabeth 6
  Richard Jr. 46
  Samuel 6, 88
Blunt,_____ 33
  (Mrs.) 10
  Ann 52
  Benjamin 46
  Priscilla 46
  Rebecca 32
  Richard 4
  Sarah 51
  William 4, 10, 32, 33, 51, 52, 53, 81, 95, 96
Boazman, Mary 1
  (Mrs.) Mary 38
  Ralph 1, 4, 38
Bocock, Martha 83, 92
  Peter 53, 83
Bococke (see Bocock)
Boddie, (Mrs.) Elizabeth 14
  John 14
  Mary 7
  William 4, 7
Bogue, William 97
Bolds, Thomas 59
Bond, John 4
  Nancy 73, 79, 95
Bones, Sampson 59, 86
Boon, James 53
  Ratcliff 5, 53
  Rebecca 84
  Selah 5
  Sion 59, 80
Booth, Mary 41
  Patience 25
  Richard 41
  Shelly 25
Borland, John 59
Boulger, Thomas 5
Bounds, Mary 85
  Thomas 60, 84, 88
Bourden, Nicholas 5
Boutcher, Elizabeth 3
Bowcock (see Bocock)
Bowden, Elias 84
  Joseph 90
  Lemuel 9
  Nancy 75
  Peggy 9
  Rhody 85
  Richard 75
Bowen, George 59
  John 4
  John Jr. 53
Bowles, Elizabeth 55
Bowzer, Dolly 59, 86

Boyce, Celia 27
  Daniel 59
  William 27
Boyd, Thomas 4, 59, 87
Boykin, Francis 4, 76
  (Mrs.) Margaret 47
  Mary 41
  Simon 70
  William 4, 47, 59
Bracey (see also Bressie)
  Campion 79
  Elizabeth 35, 102
  (Mrs.) Elizabeth 28,
    35, 38
  Francis 101
  Mary 28, 38, 102
  Sarah 82
  Sellaway 95
  Solomon 93
Bracy (see Bracey)
Braddy, Ann 32
  Mason 32
  Patrick 5, 75
  William 53
Bradley, Abraham 59
  Catherine 93
  David 5, 59, 76, 90, 95
  Henry 92
  Rhoda 85
  Samuel 5, 60, 68, 88
Bradshaw, Benjamin 72
  Elias 59
  Elizabeth 61
  George 13
  Jonas 59, 60
  Martha 13
  William 5
Bragg, Elizabeth 44
  (Mrs.) Elizabeth 40
  James 5, 15, 34, 40, 44
  Mary 34
  Sarah 15
Braise, Francis 97
  Hugh 97
Branch, Ann 24
  George 5, 24, 31
  Lucy 104
  Sarah 31
Brantley, Ann 73, 88
  Benjamin 5
  Davis 60
  Edward 5, 14
  James 83
  John 5, 48
  Mary 14, 85
  Philip 5
  Richard 89
  Sarah 74, 93
  (Mrs.) Silvia 48
  Thomas 60, 86, 92
  Unity 57, 87
  Valentine 60
  Willis 5
  Wilson 74, 83
  Winney 83, 91
Brashier (see also Bracey
  and Bressie)
  Margaret 98
  Robert 98
Brassell, John 5
Brasseur (see Braise)
Brassey, Patience 101
Brassheur (see Bracey and
  Bressie)
Brassieur (see Bracey and
  Bressie)
Braswell, Ann 2
  George 60, 90

Braswell (cont.)
  Jane 40
  Milly 92
  Rebecca 48
  Richard 40
  Robert 2, 44, 48
  Sally 73, 90
Bressie (see also Bracey)
  Elizabeth 4
  Hugh 4, 6, 97
  John 5
  Milboran 23
  Solomon 5
  Susanna(h) 6, 98
  (Mrs.) Susannah 28
  William 23, 28, 97
Bressy (see Bressie)
Brewer, (Mrs.) Ann 24
  John 5, 24
  Juliana 23
  Martha 76
  Thomas 23
Briand, Elizabeth 11
  James 11
Brickell, Mathais 5
Bridelle (see also Bridle
  and Brydle)
  Francis 14
  Mary 14
Bridger, Catherine 3
  Elizabeth 30
  Hester 51
  J. S. 70
  James 60, 73
  James Allen 60, 80
  John 5, 6, 60, 77
  Joseph 3, 6, 18, 20,
    24, 27, 30, 37, 45,
    51
  (Col.) Jos. 76
  Judith 3
  Keziah 85
  Lear 6
  Margaret 20
  Martha 27
  Mary 37, 45, 73, 76, 88
  Sally 7
  Samuel 6, 7
  Sarah 24
  (Mrs.) Sarah 18
  Susanna 80
  Tempy 70
  William 6, 60
Bridle (see also Bridelle
  and Brydle)
  Elizabeth 22
  Francis 22
Briggs, Charles 6
  David 77
  Elizabeth 54, 62, 92
  Henry 54
  James 6, 54
  James Sr. 6
  John 96
  Priscilla 54
  Sally 77, 92
Brister, Mary 60
Britt, Ann 11
  Benjamin 11, 56
Britain/Britten/Britton
  53, 60, 82, 94
  Caty 24
  Edward Sr. 6, 24
  Elizabeth 63, 104
  Holland 78, 91
  James 60
  John 6
  Joseph 60, 80

Britt (cont.)
  Sally 56
  Samuel 66
Broadfield, Charles 60
  John 60, 71, 85
Brock, Benjamin 43, 61, 89
  Elizabeth 65
  (Mrs.) Elizabeth 43
  Robert 6
  Thomas 6
  William 60
Bromfield, Ann 8
  John 6, 8, 37, 43
  Mary 43
  (Mrs.) Olive 37
Brown/Browne, (Mrs.) 36
  Catherine 83
  Edward 6, 68
  Elean 32
  Elizabeth 14, 27, 87
  G. A. 60
  George 6
  Gustavus Adolphus 93
  (Mrs.) Hester 47
  James 6, 47, 53
  Jane 91
  Jesse 6, 45
  (Dr.) Jesse 6
  John 7, 14, 36, 65
  John Jr. 60
  Joseph 60, 86
  Lucy 87
  Margaret 43
  Martha 29
  Mary 4, 15, 89
  Nancey 89
  Patty 93
  Penelope 30
  Polly 81, 91
  Ridley 45
  Robert 27, 43
  Samuel 7, 58
  (Dr.) Samuel 3, 15, 29,
    30
  Sarah 3, 32, 84, 86
  Tabitha 65, 91
  Tatty 92
  Thomas 7, 32, 53
  William 4, 7, 53
Bruce, James 7
  John 13
  (Mrs.) Mary 13
Bruin, Thomas 7
Bryan, Andrew 62, 92
  Mary 73, 91
Bryant, Charles 7, 60, 95
  Edward 7
  George 7
  John 7
  William 60, 79, 91
Brydle (see also Bridelle
  and Brydle)
  Francis 97
  Mary 97
Bufkin, Dorothy 98
  Leaven 97
Bulger, John 85
  Thomas 7
Bullard, _____ 32
  Thomas 32
Bullock, Amelia 85
  Barden 95
  Elizabeth 68, 92, 95
  John 7, 88, 90
  Joseph 7, 37
  Mary 37
  Obadiah 60
  Sarah 102

110

Garner (cont.)
 Thomas 66, 69, 75, 86
Garnes, Elizabeth 18
 John 18, 32
 Polly 91
 Sarah 32
Garrett (see also Yar-
 rett)
 Ann 102
 Catherine 100
 Elizabeth 99
 Lazarus 54
 William 99
Garton, Stephen 69
 William 19, 66
Gaskins, Thomas 19, 67,
 87
Gaston (Garton?), Wil-
 liam 92
Gay, (Mrs.) 29
 Allen 67
 Edward 85
 Everett 67
 Henry 29
 John 85
 Joshua 19, 85
 Mary 77
 Thomas 98
 William 77
George, (Mrs.) Ann 30
 Elizabeth 92
 John 30
 Rebecca 30
 Sarah 30
 (Mrs.) Sarah 3
 William 3, 19
Geruise, Thomas 19
Gibbs, Betsey 77
 Frances 85
 (Mrs.) Frances 36
 Gabriel 19, 36, 67
 John 19, 65, 67, 91
 Mary 58, 91
 Patsey 81
 Polly 57, 87
 William 19, 93
Giles, _____ 13
 Ann 33
 Elizabeth 43, 77, 88
 Ellenor 43
 Hugh 13, 19, 25, 30
 John 19, 33, 60, 77
 (Mrs.) Katherine 30
 Louisa 94
 Lucy 80
 Philarita 25
 Thomas 19, 43, 80
Gladhill, Reuben 19
Glover, _____ 6
 (Mrs.) Ann 33
 John 19
 William 6, 33
Goad, Henry 19
Godby, George 84
 Russell 85
Godfrey, Ann(e) 70, 86
 Charles 69
 Lemuel 57, 69
 Sally 69, 70, 92
 William 57, 67, 92
Godwin, _____ 16, 27, 37
 Amelia 86
 Ann(e) 17, 62, 92, 96
 (Mrs.) A-ne 55
 Betsey G. 87
 Betsey Green 79
 Brewer 19, 78
 Burgh 67

Godwin (cont.)
 Charlotte 81, 88
 Edmond/Edmund 19, 25,
 37, 39, 55, 64, 67,
 87
 Edwin 85, 95
 Elisha 67, 95
 Elizabeth 37, 39, 43,
 48, 66, 67, 94, 95
 (Mrs.) Elizabeth 4
 George 67
 James 4, 16, 20, 67,
 95
 Jeremiah 78, 87
 Jesse 91
 John 17, 48, 60, 74,
 79, 88
 Jonathan 20, 60, 67,
 96
 Joseph 37, 43, 63, 67,
 90, 92
 Kinchin 38
 Lemuel 20, 30, 40
 Margaret 25
 Martha 11, 20, 78, 87
 Mary 15, 49, 91, 92
 (Mrs.) Mary 40
 Mathew 20
 Patience 37
 Polly 67, 92
 Polly Benn 83, 91
 Rebecca 38
 Robert 20
 Samuel 15, 27, 40, 79
 Sarah 30
 (Mrs.) Sarah 10
 Sarah Bembridge 10
 Scarsbrook 62
 Silvia 66
 Silvey 81
 Sophia 40
 Thomas 20, 37, 48, 85
 William 11, 20, 49, 67,
 84, 96
 Willis 67, 95
 Wright 67, 92
Goldham, Henry 20
 Thomas 20
Goldsborough, Nicholas 20
Goodman, Martha 54
 William 54
Goodrich, (Mrs.) Anne 28
 Benjamin 72
 Edward 20, 23
 Elizabeth 20, 23
 George 8, 10, 67, 92
 Harly 86
 Honour 34
 John 13, 20, 28, 35, 61
 John Sr. 22
 Mary 8, 13
 Mesheck 93
 (Mrs.) Rebecca 22
 William 67, 68, 83, 91
Goodson, _____ 95
 Edward 20, 30
 Elizabeth 69
 Elley 77
 George 20
 James 77
 Joanna 85
 John 20, 68, 95
 Nicholas 68, 92
 Peggy 77
 Willis 68
Goodwin (see Godwin)
Gordon, Stephen 78
 William 104

Graham/Grayham, Thomas
 68, 91
Granberry, Tabitha 85
Grantham, Edward 20
Gray, Aaron 46
 Angelina 65, 91
 Ann 50, 82, 89
 Elizabeth 66, 67
 George 72, 96
 Henry 21, 54, 87
 James 68, 91, 95
 Jesse 68, 72, 82, 87
 Joseph 68, 91
 Josiah 21, 68, 91
 Mary 87
 Mourning 50
 Nancy 57, 96
 Nathaniel 68, 82, 94
 (Mrs.) Patsey 79
 Priscilla 104
 Sally 85
 Samuel 68, 90
 (Mrs.) Sarah 46
 Susanna 67
 Willis 68
Green, Bridget 39
 George 21
 Horatio 64, 68, 87
 John 11, 50
 Mary 4, 13, 50
 (Mrs.) Mary 4, 10, 31
 Peter 21
 Rachel 62, 89
 Sarah 11
 Thomas 10, 13, 21, 31,
 39
 William 21, 62
Greenwood, (Mrs.) Eliza-
 beth 37
 Thomas 37
Griffeth (see also Griffin)
 _____ 26
 Jane 15
 Owen 26
 Rowland 15
Griffin (see also Griffeth)
 _____ 15
 Andrew 28
 (Mrs.) Ann 45
 Edward 21
 Henrietta 28
 (Mrs.) Mary 4
 Mathew 21
 Michael 21
 Owen 4, 15, 21
 Patsey 93
 Shadrach 21
 Thomas 21, 45
Groce (see also Gross)
 Charles 58, 68, 74, 75,
 78, 94
 Sarah 88
 William 68, 87
 Willis 96
Gross (see also Groce)
 Francis 4, 21
 Jane 39
 Jonathan 15, 21
 (Mrs.) Mary 15
 Mary Covington 54
 Richard 21, 39
 Sarah 4
 Susannah 30
 Thomas 30, 54
Grove, George 21
 William 21
Gwaltney, Anne 86
 Elizabeth 29, 93

Gwaltney (cont.)
Freeman 93
James 65, 83, 104
Joseph 21
Lucy 83
Martha 90
Mary 85, 86
Nancy 34
Patrick 34, 59, 62, 65
Polly 93
Sally 62, 90
Simmons 68, 72
Thomas 54
William 22, 29
Gwilliam, Hincha 22
Gwin, Solomon 68

-H-

H----, Ann 58
Hadley, Ambrose 13, 22,
    64
Mary 13, 63
Hail (see Haile)
Haile,_____ 5
John 5, 22
Lydia 64, 94
Mary 99
Samuel 85
Thomas 64, 69
William 22
Haines, Edward 26
(Mrs.) Sarah 26
Hall, Ann 52, 63, 87
Felicia 99
Frederick 84
George 52, 69, 83
Isaac 22, 69
John 22, 69
Mary 66, 86, 100
Moses 98, 99
Thomas 22, 63, 69, 76,
    95
Halliford, Amelia 79
Hamilton, William 65,
    69, 78
Hampton,_____ 33
Elijah 69
(Mrs.) Elizabeth 42
John 22, 33
Mary 31
Samuel 69, 90
Thomas 22, 31, 42
Hancock, James 54, 90
John 69, 92
Mary 80, 90
Thomas 69, 70, 77, 80,
    88
Hannah, Edward 84
Hansford, Ann 3
Lewis 3
Hanson, Charles 22
Hardiman, Thomas 22
Harding, Martha 28
Sarah 21
(Mrs.) Sarah 21, 28
Thomas 96
Hardy, Deborah 55
George 22, 70
Hannah 70, 92
Isabel 32
John 11, 15, 32, 55
Lucy 11
(Mrs.) Mary 26
Olive 15

Hardy (cont.)
Priscilla 73, 89
Richard 22, 64
Sally 65
Sarah 94
Thomas 22, 26
William 69, 83, 92
Harebottle, Thomas 22
Hargrave, Elizabeth 101
Hermon 90
Jesse 22, 101
Mary 101
Samuel 101
Sarah 103
Harrell, Nancy 57
Harris,_____ 45
Alice 18
(Mrs.) Alice 43
(Mrs.) Ann 11
Edward 22
Elizabeth 60
Fanny 16
Isabella 18
James 11, 69
John 16, 18, 22, 98
Lewis 22, 23, 70, 94
Martha 26
Mary 44
(Mrs.) Mary 8
Mathew 8, 103
Michael 54
Polly 70, 90
Robert 26, 44
Thomas 23
William 45, 69, 90
Harrison,_____ 11, 49
(Mrs.) 24
Ann 1
Benjamin 85
Constance 51
Constant 9
Elizabeth 51, 59, 60,
    90
(Mrs.) Elizabeth 5
Elizabeth Hill 83, 95
Henry 23, 52, 69
John 5, 9, 23, 24, 48,
    49, 69, 73
Jordan 9
Margaret 1
Martha 83
(Mrs.) Martha 52
Mary 49
Nancy 65, 91
(Mrs.) Prudence 42, 79
Richard 42, 81
Sally 8
Sampson 54, 76, 85
Sarah 15
Shadrack 85
Susanna 48
William 1, 8, 9, 15,
    23, 49
Hart, Arthur 23
Edwin 69
Hardy 23
Lemuel 87
Mary Ridley 88
Harvey, James 69, 92
John 23
Keziah 89
(Mrs.) Keziah Mallory
    55
Mary 70
Prudence 82, 87
Harwood, Mary 15
Hatchell, Mary 94
William 23, 69, 87

Hatton, Lewis 23
Hawkins, Benjamin 69
Catherine 20
Esther 84
Mary 65, 86, 87
Priscilla 93
Samuel 20, 69
Thomas 23
Hayes, Thomas 23
Haynes, William 23
Haywood, William 23
Heath, Elizabeth 96
Isaiah 69, 76
Polly 76, 94
Robert 23, 70, 89
Hedgpeth, Elisha 70
Elizabeth 70
Henry 70
Herbert, John Markham 23
Hern, Deborah 38
Henry 38, 39
Rachel 39
Herring, Betsey 60
Daniel 70, 76, 92
Elias 60, 70
Hicks, Benjamin 63
Thomas 85
Hill,_____ 45
Bethiall 11
Elizabeth 13, 23, 80,
    87
Francis 23
Henry 23
John 13
Joseph 24
Martha 4
Mary 23, 26
Nicholas 24, 26
(Mrs.) Silvestra 4, 45
Thomas 24
William 85
Hilton, John 70, 90
Hitchens, Elizabeth 99
Hobbs, Elizabeth 85
Francis 22
Francis Sr. 24
Margaret 22
Peter 70, 86
Hockaday, John 70, 92
Hodges, Benjamin 14, 24
Ellis 23
Hartwell 14
James 91
John 24
John Jr. 24
Mary 23
Robert 24
Hodsden, Mary 66, 85, 92
William 24, 55
Hole, John 24, 37
(Mrs.) Mary 37
Holladay (see also Holli-
    day)
Anne 79
Anthony 70, 86
Elizabeth 85
Hezekiah 70, 79, 85
Jemima 89
Josiah 70, 92
Mary 74
Mills 70, 91
Patsey 67, 96
Samuel 65, 70
Thomas 70
Holland, Bethsheba 56
Benjamin 63, 76
Betsey 88
Charlotte 45, 80

113

Johnson (cont.)
  Sarah 6
  Tempy 70
  Thomas 3, 58, 60, 68, 71
  William 26, 72
  Willis 72
Johnston, James 26, 69, 72, 89
  (Dr.) Robert 26
Joiner (see Joyner)
Joliff, Scarsbrook 72, 87
Jolliff, Sally 64, 89
Jolly, John 75
  Sarah 75, 88
Jones,_____ 8
  Abaham 72
  Allen 72
  Ann 3, 25, 26, 36
  Arthur 11, 26
  Benjamin 79, 80
  Benjamin Jr. 72
  Betsey 85
  Brittain 21
  Comfort 54
  Courtney 78, 86
  Creasy 76
  David 8, 26, 62, 90
  Davis 58, 72, 93
  Edward 26
  Elberton 26
  Elizabeth 72, 85, 92
  (Mrs.) Elizabeth 17
  Esther 10
  Frances 58
  Francis 27
  Frankey 91
  Frederick 89
  Henry 72, 96
  Holland 66
  Isaac 93
  James 27
  John 3, 10, 27
  Jonathan 27
  Joseph 17, 27
  Katherine 21
  Lemuel 27, 89
  Lucy 21
  (Mrs.) Lucy 45
  Lydia 75, 90
  Martha 26
  Mary 11, 75
  Mathew 25, 27
  Nancy 58, 92
  Nathaniel 27, 72, 87, 94
  Person 72, 92
  Polly 78
  Prudence 36
  Rebecca 79
  Richard 3
  Robert 98
  Samuel 27, 36
  Sarah 17, 46
  Thomas 17, 21, 27, 72, 78, 95
  Thomas Sr. 26
  William 27, 72, 93
  Willis 27, 45, 54, 58
Jordan,_____ 38
  Ann 101
  Arthur 27
  Benjamin 103
  Betsey 77
  Billingsley 27
  Christian 100
  Dolly 53

Jordan (cont.)
  Elizabeth 20, 36, 83, 84, 86, 99
  Frances 76
  George 27
  Isham 92
  James 27, 98
  John 27, 28, 54, 69, 98
  John Jr. 83
  Jordan 86
  Joseph 28, 98
  Joshua 28, 30, 100
  Josiah 28, 38, 53, 102
  Lois 88
  Margaret 103
  Martha 69
  Mary 63, 69, 89, 90, 91, 101
  Mathew 10, 28, 98, 102
  Nancy 69
  Nicholas 72
  Patience 27
  Patsey 90
  Peggy 15, 64, 72, 84, 89, 94
  Pleasant(s) 28, 72, 102
  Polly 78, 95
  Rachel 100
  Richard 15, 27, 28, 36, 64, 98
  Robert 28, 72, 89, 94, 98, 100
  Sally 96
  (Mrs.) Sarah 30
  Thomas 72, 89, 98
  Thomas Sr. 98
  William 28, 55, 72, 83, 84
  Wilmuth 59
Joyner,_____ 81
  Bridgman/Bridgeman 7, 55
  Catherine 16, 85
  Elizabeth 7, 28
  Joseph 28
  Martha 46
  Mary 86
  Mildred 76, 95
  Sally 104
  Theophilus 28
  Thomas 16, 28, 29, 46, 69, 95
  William 28

-K-

Kae, (Mrs.) Alexandera 33
  (Mrs.) Ann 40
  Elizabeth 18
  Robert 28, 33
  Robert Sr. 18
  (Capt.) Robert 40
Kanedy, (Mrs.) 19
  Morgan 19
Keeble, Tobias 28
Kelly, Michael 73, 90
Kemp, Nancy W. 59
Kenerly, Joseph 99
Kepp(s), Cornelia 71, 87
Kimball, John 73, 80, 94
  Polly 80, 94
Kinchen (see Kinchin)

Kinchin, Elizabeth 27
  Martha 26
  Patience 45
  Sarah 20
  William 20, 26, 27, 28, 45
King, Ann 50
  Esther 52, 93
  Henry 26, 29, 55
  John 29, 52, 73
  (Mrs.) Juliana 44
  (Mrs.) Martha 8
  Robert 50
  Sally 8
  Susannah 26
  Thomas 29, 81
Kirle, Phoebe 51
  William 29
Kirle(?), Phoebe 51
Kitchen, Lydia 103
Knott, James 29

-L-

Ladd, Jesse 102
Lain, Benjamin 55
Lambeth, John 29
Lancaster,_____ 12
  Elizabeth 37
  Henry 3
  Jerusha 96
  Lucy 3
  Martha 94
  Mary 3
  Nancy 80
  Rebecca 91
  Robert 12, 37
  (Mrs.) Sarah 3
Lane, Joseph 25, 29
  Mary 8, 25
  Peggy 94
  Richard 9, 23
  Sarah 23
  Timothy 29
Lankford, Caty 17
  George 64
  Mary 71
  Stephen 17
  Thomas 29
  Wiley 73, 79
  Willis 60
Larimore, (Mrs.) Alice 47
  Roger 29, 47
Lawrence,_____ 8, 13
  Ann 3, 17, 41
  Celia 84
  Elizabeth 78
  George 36, 73, 91
  Hardy 104
  Henry 99
  Holland 69, 87
  Isabel 99
  Jeremiah 17
  Joane 98
  John 3, 8, 13, 27, 29, 41, 45, 49, 55, 73, 88, 90, 102
  Joseph 92
  Josiah 29
  Katherine 27
  Margaret 13
  Mary 45, 55, 70, 80, 88, 91
  Miles/Mills 63, 78
  Nancy 78

115

Mercer (cont.)
 Robert 55
 Thomas 32
Meredith, Joseph 32, 99
 Sampson 99
Mial, Thomas 32
Michael, Elizabeth 93
 Mary 93
Michaels, John 56
 Rose 56
Midland, George 46
 Mary 46
Middleton, Owen 32
Miller, (Mrs.) Frances 56
 John 24, 32
 Lucy 24
 (Mrs.) Lucy 24
 (Mrs.) Margaret 51
 Mary 91
 (Mrs.) Mary 24
 Nicholas 1, 32
 Polly 75
 Robert 56
 Sarah 1
 Thomas 32
 William 51
Milner, John 75
 Marth 85
 Mildred 77
Miles/Mills 74, 94
 Thomas 86
Mington, Jeptha 32
Miniard/Minyard, Joseph
 74, 91
Minton, Elias 32
Mintz, Bathesheba 84
 Edward 32
Mirick, Owen 32
Mister, Sally 68
Mitchell, James 32
Monro, (Rev.) Andrew 33
 John 7, 12, 33
 Lydia 7
 Mary 7
 Uriana 12
Montgomery, Elizabeth 9
 Hugh 66, 85
 (Mrs.) Mary 18
 Robert 18
Moody, Betty 81
 Diana 62
 Elizabeth 10
 Isaac 33, 81
 Ishmael 74, 93
 John 74
 Joseph 62, 71, 74, 81
 Mary 45
 Nancy 81, 95
 Phillip 10, 45, 93
 Polly 74, 94
 Sally 81
 Sarah 94
 William 74
Moon, Mary 21
 Thomas 21, 33
Moone (see Moon)
Moore,_____10, 49
 Aaron 94
 Elinor 37
 Elizabeth 14
 George 9, 33, 37
 Isaac 14, 47
 Jane 9
 John 9, 10, 33, 49
 Magdalen 9
 Peggy 68
 Susanna 47
 Thomas 33

Moreing, Elizabeth 88
Moreland, Ann 51, 92
 John 51
Morris, Christian 23
 Hannah 22
 James 74, 91
 Jesse 33
 John 22, 23, 44
 Sarah 44
 William 74, 93
Morrison,_____94
 James 33, 68
 John 95
 Margaret 28
 Mary 57
 Nancy 46
 Peggy 95
 William 28, 46
Moscrop,_____33
 Jane 1
 Mary 20
 Thomas 1, 20, 33
Mountford, Thomas 74
Mountfort, Mary 79, 92
 Micajah 79, 83, 95
 Nancy 83, 92
Mumford, Mary 21
 Thomas 21
Munford, Micajah 73
 Thomas 90
Munger, John 12, 33
 (Mrs.) Mary 12
Murfrey/Murphrey/Murphry/
 Murphy
 Charles 74, 94, 96
 Dempsey 74, 94
 Elizabeth 15
 Ellianor 29
 Jesse 74, 88
 John 74
 Margaret 29
 (Mrs.) Mary 31
 Michael 15, 33
 William 29, 31, 33
Murrell, George 55, 99
Murrey (see also Murry)
 Alexander 33
 Elizabeth 30
 John 33
 Mary 13, 101
 Ralph 33
 Robert 33
 Thomas 13, 30, 33
 William 33
Murry (see also Murrey)
 _____42
 Elizabeth 56
 Esther 42
 James 74
 John 56, 59, 99
 Pattey/Patty 75, 87
 Thomas 42
 Wilson 93

-N-

Nash, Hester 6
 Nicholas 6
Neavill, Tempy 73
Nelm (see Nelms)
Nelms,_____21, 26
 Ezekiel 104
 Jeremiah 34
 John 11, 21, 26, 34,
 72, 75

Nelms (cont.)
 Mary 11
 Rachel 74, 94
 William 76, 81
Nelson, Elizabeth 82
 John 75, 91
 William 34, 75
Nevelle, Ann 22
 Rachell 8
 Roger 8, 22
Nevill, Amelia 93
 John 34
 Tempy 90
 Thomas 85
Neville, (Mrs.) 43
 John 3
 Martha 3
 William 43
Newby, Ann 44
 Dorothy 97
 Joseph 102
 Nathan 99
 Thomas 44, 55
 William 97, 99
Newman, Chloe 42
 Elizabeth 57, 91
 James 34
 Jennett 77
 John 8, 34, 85
 Josiah 42
 Mary 8
 Nancy 57
 Nelly 86
 Patsey 67, 92
 Solomon 75, 90
 Thomas 34, 67, 99
Newsum, Joel 86
 Sarah 3
 Thomas 3
Niblett, Edward 34
 John 34
Nicholds,_____14
 Thomas 14
Nicholson, (Mrs.) Mariable
 39
 Richard 39
 Robert 65, 66, 75, 87
Nicolson (see Nicholson)
Nixon, Samuel 89
Nolliboy, Daniel 34
 Needham 39
 (Mrs.) Penelope 39
Norsworthy/Norseworthy
 Benjamin 96
 Charles 44
 Charlotte 16, 74, 87
 Christian 41, 74, 103
 Cittey 71
 Elizabeth 6, 33, 38, 39,
 62, 91
 Fanny 82
 Geo. 4
 George 5, 33, 34, 41, 75
 (Mrs.) Jane 54
 John 6, 34, 49, 54, 75
 Joseph 21, 34, 39, 75, 96
 Martha 5, 44, 55, 72, 79
 (Mrs.) Martha 4
 Mary 21, 22, 45
 Michael 16, 69
 Mills 82
 Nancy 87
 Nanny 80
 Patsey 88
 Peggy 62, 85
 Polly 82
 (Mrs.) Rachel 49
 Sally 18

119

Rogers, John 41, 55
Michael 96
Richard 90
Ronald, Andrew 41
Ronaldson, Patrick 41,
70
Rookings, William 41
Roper, Hugh 11
Joane 11
Rose, Lucy 44
William 44
Roseter, Ann 98
Ross, John 78
Rotchell, George 41
Roundtree, Charles 70
Rountree, Charles 95
Rudkin, William 78
Ruffin, Benjamin 41
Edward 41
Runels (see Reynolds)
Rutter, (Mrs.) Martha 1
Walter 1, 41

-S-

Samford, Thomas 41
Sampson, Ann 15
Elizabeth 10
James 10, 15, 41, 51
Margaret 51
Peter 78, 90
Sanborne, Mary 100
Sanborne/Sanbourne
Daniel 28, 100
Elizabeth 28
Sanders (see Saunders)
Sanderson, Jonathan 41
Sandifur, William 41
Saunders, Benjamin 78
Betty 8
Catherine 38
Elias 56, 80, 88
Elizabeth 39, 61,
80, 81
(Mrs) Elizabeth 16
Henry 41, 53, 61, 63,
66
Job 78
John 39, 70, 78, 81,
91
(Mrs.) Martha 53
Mary 81, 86
Robert 8, 38
Sarah 16, 80
Thomas 78
William 100
Savage, Joel 41
Sawyer, Elizabeth 48
Thomas 41
Scammell, John 41
Scott, Ann 35
Courtney 37
Elizabeth 2, 86, 98,
102
James Took 35, 41, 103
John 41, 100
Joseph 41
Mourning 12
Robert 41
Sarah 24, 102
Thomas 24, 37, 42
William 2, 12, 42,
100, 103
Seagrave, Frances 41
Francis 41, 46

Seagrave (cont.)
Lucretia 46
Seaward (see Seward)
Sebrell, Daniel 103
Lidia 103
Moses 103
Naomey 101
Segar, Nancy 65
William 65
Selden, Bartholomew 42
Sellaway, Elizabeth 1
John 1, 21, 41, 42
Margaret 41
Mary 21
(Mrs.) Mary 44
Richard 44
Selloway (see Sellaway)
Seward, (Mrs.) Mary 26
William 26, 78, 94
Sharpe,_____40
Richard 40
Shaw,_____29, 43
(Mrs.) Elizabeth 29,
43, 49
Mary 49
Shelley, Phillip 42
Shelly, Benjamin 93
John 56, 64
Mary 89
Nancy 74, 90
Sally 93
Thomas 79, 95
Shepherd, (Mrs.) 40
John 40
Samuel 42, 79
Stephen 89
Sherrer, Eleanor 45
John 45
Sherrod, John 79, 92
Shields, Mary 92
Shipley, Jonathan 42
Shivers, Betsey 86
Elizabeth 54
Jonas 42
Joseph 42, 74, 76
Peter 79, 86
Polly 59, 92
Robert 54
Sally 37
Temperance 79, 92
William 59, 79
William Sr. 37
Shumacke, Arnold 42
Sikes (see also Sykes)
Andrew 42, 80
Polly 80
Thomas 42, 100
Simmons, Ann 21, 41
Charles 42
Elizabeth 26
James 10, 21
John 26, 41
Lucy 41
(Mrs.) Lucy 4
Mary 10, 17, 103
Stephen 4, 17
Simms, John 42
Sims, Charles 42
Sinclair, John 43
Skelton, Elizabeth 46
Thomas 46
Skinner, Arthur 43
Elizabeth 39
Mary 54
Richard 39
Slease(?), William 86
Small, Amey 97
Benjamin 97, 100

Small (cont.)
John 100
Joseph 100
Smelley, Ann 55
(Mrs.) Eleanor 19
Elizabeth 28
Jean 52
John 43, 52, 55
Lewis 28, 43
Patsey 17
Robert 43
Sally 68
Sarah 94
Thomas 43
William 17, 19, 43
Smelly (see Smelley)
Smith,_____24, 38
(Mrs.) 35
Ann 17, 35, 48, 76
(Mrs.) Ann 2, 31
Arthur 3, 6, 14, 24,
33, 40, 43, 61
Betsey 44
Elizabeth 26, 35, 65,
72, 93
Holland 76
James 43, 88
Jane 3, 40
Jenny 73, 94
John 43, 76, 84
Joseph 9, 24, 37, 43,
79, 84
Joseph Jr. 61
Joseph Sr. 79
(Mrs.) Leodowick 59
Martha 6, 14
Mary 24, 31, 54, 61
(Mrs.) Mary 9, 35, 37
Nancy 67
Nicholas 31, 35, 38,
79, 85, 94
Olive 24
Pamelia 66, 86
Robert 43
Samuel 64, 72, 79, 94,
95, 96
Sarah 5, 7, 60
Stephen 67, 75, 79, 87
Thomas 26, 31, 56, 72,
79, 86
Virgus 54
William 5, 7, 35, 43,
48, 88
William Rand 67, 79
Willis 79
Snowden, Richard 43
Sojurnour, John 43
Southall, James B. 56
Spence, Elizabeth 31
William 31
Spencer, Peggy 66
Spiltimber, Anthony 25, 44
Martha 25
Spyvie, Benjamin 44
Stallings, John 44
Joseph 65, 75, 79
Lucy 83
William 79, 84, 93
Stamp, Samuel 96
Stantlin, Darby 44, 47
(Mrs.) Julian 47
Stanton, James 44
Staples,_____40
Richard 40
Stephenson (see also
Stevenson)
Edmund 56
Elizabeth 44

120

Vasser, Elizabeth 8
  Nathan 8
  Peter 8
Vaughan, Adah 66
  Francis 58, 71
  Henry 46
  James 66, 81
  Peggy 66
  Thomas 47
  Uriah 66
Vellines, Caty 38
  Isaac 81, 94, 95, 96
  John 86
  Nathaniel 47, 69
  Twaite 38, 47
Vicars, (Mrs.) Jane 8
  John 8
Vickers, Margaret 4
  Ralph 4
Vivian, Thomas 47

-W-

Wade, Samuel 47
Waikley, Mathew 47
Wail, Nancy 61
Waile, _____ 21
  Josiah 84
  Nicholas 21
Wainwright, _____ 50
  Elizabeth 54
  Mary 42
  Sarah 33
  William 33, 42, 47,
    50, 54
Wakefield, John 42, 47
  Sarah 42
  Thomas 47
Walden, William 74
Walker, George 47
Wallace, Celia 61, 91
Waller, Benjamin 84
  Mary 59
Walters, Walter 47
Waltham, William 68
Walton, John 47
Ward, Ann 72
  Benjamin 39, 65, 85
  Elizabeth 44
  Frances 9
  John Wiatt 47
  Joseph 44
  Martha 85
  Mary 57, 91
  (Mrs.) Mary 10
  Nancy 72
  Olive 10
  Rebecca 41
  (Mrs.) Sarah 39
  Thomas 9, 10, 41, 47
  William 47
Wardroper, John 47
Warren, David 47
  Elizabeth 90
  James 89
  Jane 23
  John 47
  (Mrs.) Margaret 47
  Martha 23
  Mary 53
  Patience 27
  Robert 47
  (Mrs.) Sarah 50
  Thomas 23, 27, 50, 53
Washborne, Daniel 34

Washborne (cont.)
  Mary 34
Washington, Arthur 1
  Elizabeth 1
  Mary 1
Waters, Daniel 47
  Mary 99
  Walter 99
Watkins, _____ 17
  Ann 101
  Catherine 84
  Elianor 25
  Jesse 56, 83
  John 17, 25, 39, 63,
    73, 77
  Martha 56, 71, 88
  Mary 17, 103
  Mourning 39
  Patience 63
  Rebecca 83
  Robert 60, 65
  Sally 65
  William 47
Watson, _____ 45
  (Mrs.) Ann 37
  James 48, 55
  John 45, 47
  Martha 55
  Michael 56
  Robert 37
  William 81
Watts, John 38, 48
  Sarah 38
Waugh, John 48
Webb, _____ 34
  Elizabeth 50
  (Mrs.) Elizabeth 52
  James 34, 48, 50, 52,
    81
  Mathais 56
  Mathew 48
  Patsey 56
  Samuel 48, 80, 81
  William 48
Weeks, John 81, 95
Welch, John 48, 53
  Sarah 53
  William 48
Wentworth, Ann 7
  Betty 14
  Frances 39
  Lois 51
  Mary 37
  Samuel 7, 14, 37, 39,
    48, 51
West, _____ 22
  Francis 22
  Henry 48
  Jacoby 48
  Mary 21
  Nicholas 47, 48
  Ralph 62, 68, 74
  Richard 48
  (Mrs.) Sarah 47
  Sylvia 72
  William 21, 48, 94
Wescott, Fanny 91
Weston, Benjamin 48, 79,
    81, 88
  John 48
  Rhoda 96
  Samuel 81, 95
Westray, Arthur 48
  Benjamin 48
  Chloe 89
  Jeremiah 66
  John 49
  Levi 81

Westray (cont.)
  Mills 69
  Rebecca 66, 92
  Robert 55
  Sally 55, 69, 77
  Simon 81, 86
Wheadon, James 14, 48
  John J. 68
  Joseph 49
  Martha 14, 18
  Mary 8
  Phillip 49
Wheeler, Jacob 81
Whitaker, Dudley 81, 91
  Phineas 49
White, Anthony 49
  Elizabeth 42, 102
  Frances 68, 91
  John 42, 49, 100
  Joshua 103
  Mary 104
  Rachel 102
  Sally 87
  Samuel 49
  Shelly 79, 81, 91
  Thomas 49, 100
  William 81
Whitehead, Arthur 49
  Arthur Jr. 27
  Isabel 60
  Jesse 63, 81, 86
  Joseph 49
  Lewis 103
  Mary 63, 101
  (Mrs.) Patience 27
Whitfield, Abraham 36
  Ann 15
  (Mrs.) Ann 12
  Catey 64
  Copeland 81, 82, 89, 90
  Copeland Jr. 82
  Elizabeth 36
  (Mrs.) Elizabeth 15
  Fanny 73
  (Mrs.) Fanny 29
  Jemima 85
  Kerenhappuck 16
  Margaret 102
  Mary 56, 64, 91
  Mathew 49
  Polly 57
  Priscilla 64, 90
  Samuel 29, 49, 82
  Thomas 16, 49, 56
  William 49
  Wilson 56, 61, 75
Whitley, Betsey 61
  Bracey 84
  Catherine 84
  Elizabeth 71, 78, 88,
    94
  Emily 60
  George 82, 93
  Ishmael 82
  John 49
  John Saunders 82, 94
  Joseph 49
  Mills 82
  Nathan 61
  Randall 82
  Randolph 82
  Tabitha 59, 78, 82
  Thomas 49
  Timothy 82
  William 82, 94
Wiggs, Catherine 56
  Elizabeth 97
  George 1, 9

Wiggs (cont.)
Henry 50, 56, 97, 100
(Mrs.) Mary 1
Sarah 9
William 103
Wilds, (Mrs.) Ann 11
Thomas 11, 50
Wilkinson, Ann 2
(Mrs.) Ann 18
Cofer 82
Cofield 50
Easter 24
Elizabeth 46, 53, 85,
102
Henry 53, 100
(Mrs.) Martha 34
Mary 36
Rachel 35, 50, 93
Richard 2, 20, 24, 35,
36, 46, 50
William 18, 50, 85, 100
Willis 34, 82
Wilkinson(?), Elizabeth
20
Willet, Betsey 86
Fanny 85
Williams_____3, 7, 24,
27, 38
(Mrs.) 16
Ann 38, 102
(Mrs.) Ann 42
Arthur 16, 50
David 50, 82, 87
Dennis 50
Elizabeth 13, 40, 52
Ellen 41
Epaphroditus 50, 52
George 40, 50
Jacob 50
James 93
John 16, 24, 38, 42,
50, 52, 56
John Sr. 7
Jones 41
Jordan 82
Julia 95
Juliana 52, 63
Letitia 67, 90
Martha 101
Mary 62, 93
(Mrs.) Mary 27
Nancy 69, 92
Peter 50
Priscilla 16
Prudence 70
Richard 13, 50, 64, 67,
69
Rowland 3
Thomas 50
William 50
Williamson_____13
Arthur 50
Burwell 28
Elizabeth 47
Francis 38, 51
Geo. 4
George 13, 17, 51
Hester 4
James 51
(Mrs.) Jean 8
(Mrs.) Margaret 16
Martha 38
Patience 17
Richard 16
Robert 51
(Dr.) Robert 8
Thomas 51
Wilmouth 28

Willis, Elizabeth M. 58
Robert 82
Wills, Barsheba 63, 91
Elizabeth 67, 80
(Mrs.) Elizabeth 19
Elvira 82
Emanuel 64
Francis 60, 64
Holland 67, 87
James 58, 63, 64, 80
John 7, 51, 82
John Jr. 23
John Scarsbrook 63, 67,
82
Josiah 77, 82
Lois 93
(Mrs.) Lois 19
Martha 21, 57, 65
(Mrs.) Martha 40
Mathew 19, 82
Miles/Mills 19, 21, 51,
57, 62, 64, 65, 68
Miles Jr. 63
Moses 56
Nathaniel 82, 91
Pamelia 82, 89
Parker 51
Polly 81, 91
(Mrs.) Prudence 23
Sally Godwin 68, 91
(Mrs.) Sarah 7
Thomas 40, 51, 60, 74,
82
Willis 51, 88, 93, 95,
96
Wilson,_____48
(Mrs.) 5
Ann 43, 59, 74, 93
Elizabeth 15, 88
(Mrs.) Frances 51
George 1, 2, 12, 15,
36, 43
Goodrich 51, 82
Honour 36
(Mrs.) Honour 37
James 37, 51, 59, 85
Jane 21
Joan 19
John 5, 21, 51
Josiah 51, 83
(Mrs.) Judith 12
Mary 2, 3, 12
Nicholas 51
(Mrs.) Prudence 33
Randall 83
Ridley 1
Robert 83
Sampson 3, 12, 64, 83,
91
Samuel 48, 51
Solomon 83, 86
Thomas 92
William 19
Willis 51
Winborne, Esther 89
John 51
Winbourne, Julia 86
Woddrop, Alexander 54,
56
Ann 54
Elizabeth 54
Wollard, (Mrs.) Elizabeth
27
Henry 27
Womble (see also Wombwell)
80
Britain/Britton 54, 55,
56, 72

Womble (cont.)
Chace(y) 54, 90
Charlotte 94
Conny 54
Elizabeth 54, 103
Frankey 91
Harty 55, 73
John 16, 66
Joseph 54
Lemuel 96
(Mrs.) Lucy 16
Mary 84
Samuel 66
William 80, 95
Wilmuth 73
Wombwell (see also Womble)
Ann 44
Britton 59, 64, 71
Celia 2
Charity 61
Charlotte 64
Edwin 61
Elizabeth 22
Jeremiah 83, 92
John 83
Joseph 52
Lemuel 52, 83
Lucy 76
Margaret 31
Mary 31
Mourning 44
Temperance 71
Thomas 2, 22, 31, 44,
56, 83, 92
William 64
Wood,_____7
Elizabeth 56
George 2
John 56, 100
Jonathan/Jonothan 83,
92
Josias 5, 7
Margaret 5, 100
Mary 2
Woodley, Andrew 11, 75,
79, 83, 95
John 53
Mary 11
Molly 53
Samuel 63
Tomas 51
Woodwide, John 51
Woodrop, Lilly 87
Woodson, Joseph 56, 100
Woodward, (Mrs.) Esther 9
John 93
John G. 9
John George 52
Peter 84
Philaretus 19
Thomas 19
William 52, 83, 85, 86
Woory, (Mrs.) Elizabeth 6
Joseph 6, 52
Wooten (see Wootten)
Wootten, Benjamin 88
John 83, 86
Richard 52
Wormeley, James 82
Worrell, John 93
Richard 52
Wrench, Elinor 34
(Mrs.) Elizabeth 27
John 27, 34, 84
Wrenn, Ann 32
Cherry 90
Francis 51, 52, 83
James 83

123

Wrenn (cont.)
  John 5, 52, 83, 86
  Josiah 52, 58, 76
  Martha 70, 91
  (Mrs.) Martha 51
  (Mrs.) Mary 32
  Polly 76, 94
  (Mrs.) Prudence 5
  Sally 58
  Thomas 52, 72
  William 89
Wright, (Mrs.) 12
  Ann(e) 21, 59, 64, 89
  Edward 60
  Elizabeth 20
  (Mrs.) Elizabeth 7
  George 15
  Henry 83
  John 8, 52
  Joseph 52
  Mathew 83, 91
  Sarah 8
  Thomas 7, 12, 20, 21, 52
  (Mrs.) Violet 15
  William 52
Wynne, (Mrs.) Elizabeth 47
  Hugh 47, 52

-Y-

Yarrett (see also Garrett)
  Elizabeth 33
  William 33
Young,_____69
  Ann 27
  Bennett 17, 27, 32, 59,
    64, 76, 82, 83, 91
  David 69
  Elizabeth 10, 36
  Frances 91
  Francis 57, 58, 59, 60,
    61, 62, 65, 66-78, 80,
    81, 83
  Francis Jr. 58, 59, 64,
    65, 68, 69, 70, 73,
    75, 77, 80, 82
  Francis Sr. 80
  James 61, 62, 70, 83,
    90
  John 36
  Nathaniel 77
  Peyton 70, 71, 73, 74
  (Mrs.) Polly Benn 32
  Rebecca 17

124

CPSIA information can be obtained at www.ICGtesting.com
Printed in the USA
BVOW082011111212

307932BV00005B/179/P

9 780806 307107